Also by the same Author

The Great Con

Salute Goliath!

A fresh look at the Bible, with conscience as our guide

by

Kennedy

*With thanks to my pupils, past and present,
for all their enthusiasm and love.*

*Keep on thinking, and trust your own judgments.
Treat ALL people well, not just some.*

Published in 1999 by MARION BOOKS
P.O. Box 28207
Edinburgh
EH9 1WL

Copyright Kennedy, 1999
ISBN 0-9536291-0-4

Typeset & Printed by
The Print Consultancy - 0131 667 5549

SALUTE GOLIATH!

INTRODUCTION

The Church's traditional teaching on the Bible can no longer be sustained. Whether Roman Catholic, Protestant or Orthodox, all hold the Old and New Testaments as "holy", and base their doctrines upon a facile reading of these books.

From Genesis to Revelation the Church has presented a view of God - or rather, a *distortion* of God - from the untenable standpoint that God chose *one* nation, and gave them licence to kill the inhabitants of a Land he would give them (and not criticise or punish when they took *more* land than that promised, and killed *more* people), and that, eventually, he would send his Son to be born of this killer nation, to show his love for *all mankind* and be their Saviour!

This ridiculous theology is still the stuff of Christian doctrine. It is high time for it to be challenged. Liberation Theology, which has become a popular concept, when applied to the politics of Latin America, must now be extended to *all* oppressed people, and to The Bible itself!

Here, I present an alternative interpretation of familiar Bible passages and characters, applying the standards of *common morality*, which are the standards of Liberation Theology. In case it is claimed that this is applying *modern* standards to a period of time, thousands of years ago, when such standards did not apply, I will point out here that such a contention cannot be sustained, and for this reason - that the nations vilified in the Bible, accused of being disgusting and abominable, fit only for *extermination* by people claiming to be *moral paragons* - those *libelled* people are the ones who show decency, civility, kindness, hospitality and a level of morality *beyond the ken* of the nation that calls itself "holy" - so much so, that even the writers of the book, in spite of all their derogatory insinuations, are not able to hide this truth.

It is a scandal that the Church, for two thousand years, has condoned a *holocaust on Canaan*, and called those who inflicted it "righteous", "people of God", and "holy". In no other context are leaders and religions, which incite and commit massacre, eulogised. In Christianity, however, it is done - and Christians are hopelessly confused by their inner voice, their conscience, which tells them, "This is wrong", and the teaching they receive in Church, which tells them, "This is right".

Which is right - Church teaching or conscience? Why, *conscience*, of course!

CHAPTER 1

LIBERATION THEOLOGY

Liberation Theology says that God is on the side of the victims of oppression, and *not* of the oppressor. It accords with our innate sense of justice, and with the teaching in Jesus' Sermon on the Mount (Matthew 5). As a religious and political movement, it began in Latin America in the 1960s, when priests, siding with the poor, started to speak out against the injustices of right-wing regimes, and to call for human, civil and social rights for the downtrodden, exploited classes. Whilst the activists became popular with the poor, they offended those in power, the rich, who also owned most of the land. In the Roman Catholic Church they, at first, also faced opposition from the Church hierarchy, who wished to keep in with those in power. Thousands of clergy and lay people, who spoke out and took action on behalf of the poor, were arrested, kidnapped, interrogated, and tortured. Many were murdered for the stance they took. To dare to speak out for land reform, for example, or try to get trade unions formed for the benefit of workers, was to hazard your life. The murderers were hardly ever brought to book.

As news of what was happening became known in the wider world, ordinary church members thought Liberation Theology was a really good thing. Brave journalists reported, Amnesty International took up cases and causes, Christian charities sent aid, TV made films about "The Disappeared" - all of which helped to jolt public opinion, and democratic governments, to begin to put pressure on right-wing governments to start taking measures to make life better for their poor, exploited underclasses, and, at least, curb the worst violations of human rights.

A tide of awareness swept the world, as country after country, government after government came under scrutiny from populations that had started to think in a more objectively critical way, not only about other regimes, but also their own. In the 1980s, Peace and Justice groups grew up in the churches of the west. People had begun to hear about the UN Charter on Human Rights, which had been drawn up in 1948, yet had not been much heeded over decades. Only now, at the very end of the 20th century, have governments started to take the Charter more seriously, and think of basing all their policies and laws on it.

It is now time to apply Liberation Theology, which is, in fact, *common morality*, to the *Bible*. This means that, instead of taking at face value the comments and

1

views of the writers, we apply the moral standards that we apply to the rest of life, and say, "Terrorism and genocide are wrong, and just because the murderers wrote some of the Bible, saying it was right, that does not *make* it right. Those things are *always wrong.*"

Our theologians need to apply themselves to the task of reinterpreting what is written in the book they call "holy", and tell us what exactly *is* holy in it, for our God-given consciences tell us that what they have told us so far about God, is a conglomeration of creator and lover of all mankind, but also cruel tyrant who loves one nation, and wants others wiped from the face of the Earth! The mental gymnastics needed to see this purveyor of hate as the fountain of love, is a contortion that church members should no longer be called upon to do.

What happens when you apply Liberation Theology to the Bible? The Old Testament, with its blood-thirsty God of drowning, and of sacrifices that make wicked people feel good - this *God of hate and war* is seen for what he is. And what is he? - A *convenience*, a *pretence* of God, in order to justify the unjustifiable. Sure - belief in him helped the heroes of the book to do the near impossible - but only because the *belief* goaded them into being more *ruthless and determined* than normal people usually are. Doubtless the leaders believed what they were telling the Israelite nation, as they psyched their warriors up, to do their bidding - but they could only have been under a grievous delusion.

CHAPTER 2

THE HITCH HIKER'S GUIDE TO CHRISTIANITY?

In a typically hilarious chapter of Douglas Adams' "trilogy", THE HITCH HIKER'S GUIDE TO THE GALAXY, the computer, Deep Thought, after a search of seven and a half million years, gives the answer to The Ultimate Question of Life, the Universe and Everything, as "forty-two". The crazy-sounding answer becomes even crazier when the questioners realise they do not even know what the question is. Even Deep Thought cannot provide them with the question! What it *can* do is design the Ultimate Computer, which, after another ten million years (and a thousand jokes), comes up with the Ultimate Question as being, "What do you get if you multiply six by nine?"

The TV version of THE HITCH HIKER'S GUIDE had the characters, Ford and Arthur philosophising that it was no wonder everything in life went wrong. Not only the whole fabric of human existence, but the whole cosmic order was built on a miscalculation! That explained an awful lot! Things are bound to go wrong, if the premise is wrong.

Christianity is based on a similar false premise, only, here it is *not* funny, but tragic. It is built on the ridiculous idea that the cruel God who inspired massacre after massacre of millions of people by one favoured nation, is also the kind, compassionate lover of all mankind. The illogic of this is plain, yet the Church will not see it. In amazing contortions of lies presented as *truth*, it has insisted down the years, that the God of Creation, who is unchanging, changes his mind about his creation being good, and drowns nearly everything and everyone. This Originator of Morality does *not* want people to be moral beings, but unthinking automatons. This God, who is supposed to want his creation "to enjoy him for ever", according to the Church's Catechism, puts a *guard* on the Garden of Eden, in case his creatures eat the fruit from the Tree of Life, *and live forever*!

The God of the New Testament is a confusion of the cruel, partisan God of the Old, and a kind, merciful, loving-all-mankind God. Jesus may have praised Abraham, Isaac and Jacob, in keeping with the religion in which he was brought up, but his teaching of God was radically different from that of his religion, as his compatriots knew. It was those *despised* by his religion, who were his main followers, although, living in that society, they had to kowtow to the religion. For example, healed "lepers" *had* to show themselves to the priests, else they could not have become part of society again.

3

Jesus reacted against many of the harsh written laws, like the stoning to death of women caught in adultery (or poisoned, just for being *suspected* of it by a silly, or devious, husband - Numbers 5 v 11-31!) yet he went along with the terrible belief in Hell, as a place of punishment for sinners in an eternally burning fire - only, Jesus' definition of "sinners" was different from the official religious one. By *his* definition, the religious people could be "sinners", if they were hypocrites. But to the Scribes, Pharisees, Sadducees and Priests, "Sinners" formed that class in society which did not fastidiously keep all the rules of the religion, particularly the praying and fasting. Hell was not an Old Testament concept, but it was an easy step to it from the harshness of Old Testament punishments, and the belief in Sheol, a shady place under the Earth, where the souls of the dead went, before finally expiring.

Although in 1860, several enlightened clergymen of the Church of England published the view that belief in Hell is untenable, the Church has never had the courage to renounce this doctrine that is firmly entrenched in the teaching of Jesus. It is high time it did so. Roughly stated, their view was, "If I, with all my imperfections, could not consign even my worst enemy to Hell, how could a perfect God do so?"

Christian ministers sometimes describe the Bible as "God's blueprint for living", advocating it as the *perfect guide,* that each of us could do no better than follow in our lives. If we did, we might learn to be harsh, vindictive, murdering those we despised, and expecting to get off with it, because we tell them "God told us to". We might also expect to benefit from the proceeds of our crimes, as "God's People" in the Bible did, and still do!

At the same time, we could talk of brotherly love, peace and justice for all, *and not see any disparity between our words and our actions* - that is what we could learn to be like from the Bible! To be inconsistent in our words and our actions - *that* is what we could most easily learn from the Bible. The Church tries to gloss over discrepancies, by saying that the picture of God is progressive. Yet it still teaches that some of the greatest crimes against humanity, the genocide in Canaan, were God's will! The concept of Hell, as the burning of conscious people for ever in fire, is a crime against morality - and this idea is not in the Old Testament, only in the New, in the teaching of Jesus. *That* is hardly progress!

It will not do! The Bible is *no* blueprint for living. Our God-given conscience is our only reliable guide for living. Religions claim we need rules. But religions break their very own rules with impunity. Religions distort conscience, and then disparage it. Religions say, "Do as *we* tell you. You must *not* think for yourself!" They are power mechanisms. Do *not* trust organised religions to do your thinking for you! Think for yourself! Above all, listen to your *conscience*! Let *it* be your guide!

CHAPTER 3

CONSCIENCE: GOD WITHIN US

"Our conscience, which is God."

(LES MISERABLES: Victor Hugo)

Some people say that we need to have a set of dogmas to define our morality and to live by, otherwise we would not be able to know right from wrong, for, they say, certain people think some things are right, which others think are wrong. The people who claim that we need, for example, The Ten Commandments to tell us right from wrong are entirely *mistaken*. How can I make such an assertion? Very easily! The Old Testament contains all the evidence we need. The people who received and passed on The Ten Commandments went straight from receiving them, to being the most pitiless and remorseless murderers around. And Christianity, which also claimed to live by The Ten Commandments, bred warmongers, who, on their Crusades of the Middle Ages, massacred men, women and children in the name of their religion. Having a moral code helped them not a whit. They broke every tenet of the moral code *and did not notice!* In fact, *religion* damaged their conscience so much that they could not tell right from wrong! This needs to be clearly understood, and should be a cause of *huge* concern to theologians, who have not yet given their attention to this worrying fact - *religion can seriously damage your conscience*! Neither the Crusaders nor the Church saw murder and massacre as wrong!

Codes of behaviour and rules only seem to give people a misplaced sense that, since they have *heard* them, and mentally *assented* to them, they can thereafter do no wrong. Their conscience no longer seems to function properly. Dogmas confuse people, and set one culture against another. Left to our ourselves, without rules, codes and dogmas, we would *know* right from wrong - for our *conscience* tells us that we should treat other people well, because we would like them to treat us well. God has given us this *gift*, this conscience, this *knowledge within* that we should "do as we would be done by". It is also what Bible-based religions pay lip-service to, in their teaching of, "Love your neighbour as yourself". The "Holy War" of the Old Testament, and the Crusades of the Church of the Middle Ages are *incompatible* with that teaching. They were vicious wars on peaceful people, with religion used to *quell* conscience.

Self-assertive people, who do *not* treat others well, but insist on being first, having most, or the best, will always exist. Dogmas, commandments, and rules do not make them conform. They look for chances to break them. Nor do dogmas, commandments and rules make people *good*. People can obey with ill grace. Even selfish and greedy people, and bullies recognise good and bad - they *object* when *they* are treated unfairly, or are bullied themselves. If they are to be cured of their unsocial behaviour, it is more likely to be through appealing to their conscience, than by giving them a list of *do's and don'ts*. Some schools have found this to be the case, as they attempt to deal with the problem of bullying. By getting the bully involved in dialogue with the bullied, the bully is able to see and admit that bullying is wrong. They would not like to be on the receiving end of the treatment they mete out, and thus are able to learn a better way of behaving.

Religious or nonreligious, *conscience* is apt for either type of person. To the religious, conscience is God within: to the non-religious, conscience is the human capacity to recognise good and evil. People need to learn to respect others because they are people, too, who should be valued as much as they, themselves, would like to be valued. Such a value system has no hidden agendas of adherence to one religion or another, which brings a pack of additional beliefs, duties, and inflexible traditions, which all too often impede advancement in ways of regarding others, and in ways of living. Conscience bestows common sense, as well as morality, and also self-esteem, along with esteem of others. It would certainly bring a whole trail of life-enhancing outcomes, if the nurture of conscience, rather than dogma, was paramount in religion. "Treat others as you would like them to treat you" is simple to understand. If put into practice on a personal level, one's appreciation of one's friends, acquaintances, colleagues, would enhance all one's relationships. Quarrelling, griping, backbiting would die out. One's daily round would become much more pleasurable. At community and national levels, welfare systems would be able to provide better services, for cheating would stop, leaving funds available for their proper uses. Cheating "the system" is stealing from the needy, the sick and the disabled. People would see it as such, when they learned to respect their conscience, and live by its precepts. At international level, war would be no more. The money, materials and energy, which are *enormous* and which are wasted on weapons that bring death and destruction, would all be freed for constructive and beneficial uses that could transform the lives of everyone - if only we would admit that every other person deserves the same treatment as we ourselves like.

Cultivating one's *conscience* should be highest on our personal list of priorities for our lives. Whatever life is about, it is *not* about making money, or being famous. Each of us arrives in this world with a genetic make-up, which gives us certain aptitudes, susceptibilities, and predisposes us to a certain personality, even to certain illnesses. Our personality and our health may be, to a large extent, and, in some cases, completely, outwith our control, but our *character* is not. It is *ours* to form. It is what we end up with at the end of our life, and it is built from the choices we make in our lives. We *choose* to follow good examples or bad, to do right or wrong, to treat others well or badly. We form our own character.

We need to *cultivate* our conscience. People hardly seem to feel shame, even when they do shameful things. Some hardly seem to feel guilt, even when they do bad things. (I am talking about ordinary people, not those psychologically classed as amoral.) Why not? It is time we took more interest in the *moral* aspect of our lives, and valued our conscience.

Sadly, our modern Western culture of "anything goes" and "I'll do what I want - hang everybody else", with media glorification of immoral lifestyles, and crooks as heroes, has done us the disservice of teaching us to ignore our conscience, or despise it as being "uncool", fuddy-duddy. This is disastrous to our personal and social lives. People who do not value either their own lives or others', are in danger of violating both.

This is the most important challenge to our generation: we must recover *conscience*. We must learn to *nurture* it, not disparage it. We must learn to *value* it, not debase it. We must learn to *treasure* it above anything else we treasure. Conscience is what makes us distinctly human. We are spiritually stunted if we do not listen to, and live by it. It is our spiritual part. If we think that spirituality is anything, apart from conscience, we are mistaken. Cultivating conscience is the only spirituality there is. Religious fervour is not spirituality.

But what about *guilty* conscience? *That* can be very uncomfortable, sometimes even oppressive. Remember that a conscience that can feel guilt and shame is a healthy one! Those who feel no guilt or shame for the wrong they do - and those are often *religious* people and *religious institutions* - are the most fearsome of all groups in society. For the person who feels the guilt of sin, "the penitent sinner", as the Church terms it, there is the love, forgiveness and acceptance by God, as taught and shown by Jesus. Some churches insist on an understanding of Christ as the Sacrificial Lamb, whose blood was shed for the remission of sin, as Jesus himself taught at The Last Supper, paralleling the blood sacrifices of the Old Testament. God, the Righteous Judge, requiring that *someone* be pronounced *guilty* for sin, and Jesus becoming *our substitute*, condemned in our place, is another version of why Jesus died on the Cross, taught in some churches. Christ the Redeemer, buying us back from the rule of *the Devil*, like a pledge from a pawn shop, is another, reminiscent of the old teaching on The Fall of Man".

All of those ways of describing the significance of Christ' death on the Cross hark back to, and depend on, the dubious religiosity of The Old Testament. Far better, in my view, is to stop imbuing Christianity with Old Testament religion, and admit that all too often we do wrong. We are apt to be lazy, greedy, selfish, mean, hard-hearted, spiteful and/or a hundred other things. We shun *good*, just as Jesus was shunned, and ended up on the Cross. Jesus' *teaching* is far better to cling to than stories of *blood* cleansing from sin. It is surely *enough* that God forgives the sorry sinner. Performing religious rituals may be enjoyable and edifying for some people, but it is the *knowledge* that God loves and accepts us, sinful though we are, that brings healing and comfort to bruised souls and those mourning the loss of loved ones. *That* knowledge brings with it unexpected benefits. It revives our sagging spirits, reactivates our dulled conscience, renews our energy. Thus, *guilty* conscience is a springboard for better behaviour in the future. To know oneself unworthy yet *loved by God*, and *forgiven*, is a healthful and invigorating experience. To be freed from the burden of guilt, is to be emancipated, able to think, feel and act, in a new way, reinvigorated.

Try to envisage the difference that would come about in society if *conscience* dictated our daily round, community relations, national life and international dealings! Instead of the aimlessness and purposeless that lead many people into the downward spiral of self-gratification, where pursued pleasures become ever more joyless, they could experience positive feelings of self-respect and respect for others, that would bring a new lease of life, with unexpected enjoyment of simple things. Community life would be enhanced as friends, neighbours and acquaintances received the morale-booster of mutual, positive appreciation. National life would benefit from its citizens being happier individuals, and less disposed to indulge in quarrelling and crime. International relations would improve as the practice caught on, of individuals and nations learning to treat others as they themselves liked to be treated. As distrust, fear and crime waned, life would become better and better.

Nurture of our conscience should be the prime concern in each of our lives, and in bringing up and educating children.

CHAPTER 4

THE LETTER TO THE HEBREWS

This book of the New Testament, a letter by an unknown Christian to encourage Jewish Christians in their new-found faith, is full of sickening stuff, with the worst chapter, 11, dished up in churches in Scotland as the food for the soul - the main reading and subject of sermons - on Remembrance Sunday each November. But it is only appropriate for people who wish to *glorify war*, or claim "Holy War", or try to justify war. The heroes named were aggressors, *not* defendants. Most of them - Moses, Rahab, Gideon, Barak, Samson, Jephthah, David, Samuel - colluded in mass-murder, some of them wielding weapons themselves! (Why did the writer omit Joshua?) This letter praises all of them as carrying out God's directions to implement an Old Covenant, a promise of a Land and many descendants, in return for obedience. Obedience soon came to mean killing animals for religious purposes, instead of just for food, and killing millions of people as well!

The Christian Church has this letter as scripture because it makes the claim, right at the outset, that Jesus is the fulfilment of Old Testament prophecy, and is therefore "The Messiah", the longed-for Jewish leader, who would lead the nation to the pinnacle of world power and domination. The very first verses of the Letter make the points that *God* spoke to their ancestors, often, in the past, and, in many ways, through the prophets - but his most recent communication has been through *his Son*. It was through him that God created the universe, and sustains it. He is like God in glory and power. He achieved forgiveness for the sins of mankind, and now he sits on a throne at God's right hand! "How does he know *that*?" we ought to ask.

Quoting extensively from the Psalms, as well as from the Law and Prophets, the writer rams his point home, that the Old Testament was *all* leading to Jesus. Christ's death on the Cross was in complete accord with the sacrificial system instituted by Moses, being, the writer claims, the *final* sacrifice for sin, the fulfilment of the Old Covenant, and the implementation of the New.

By making the claim that the Old Covenant leads to Jesus, Christianity validates the barbaric religion and unjustifiable claims of the Old Testament. It accepts the precept that everything Abraham and Moses wanted was what God directed - *and this is totally ridiculous!* The Church *must* begin to apply some moral discernment and judgment to what it teaches. It must re-evaluate its doctrines.

10

In short - it is time to apply the standards of Liberation Theology to the Bible, and to Christian teaching. Christian double-speak will no longer do!

The following chapters indicate the kind of new thinking that needs to be applied to both the Old and New Testaments, but especially to the Old, whose murdering heroes are *kept as heroes* in the New. The Letter to the Hebrews commends the great faith of mythical characters, like Abel, Enoch and Noah - and has a great amount to say about Melchizedek, of whom practically *nothing* is known. But a shortage of facts does not deter the writers of the Bible from pushing their views, and *we need to think hard* before accepting them.

By applying common sense and common morality to the Bible, I challenge its verdict on the heroes of the faith.

CHAPTER 5

THE CREATION OF THE UNIVERSE IN GENESIS 1

"In the beginning..."(v 1)

Scientifically speaking, there could not be a beginning of *everything*, for, if there was ever *nothing*, nothing would remain; there could only be a beginning of the universe, as we know it, through a change in *something* that was before. This means that eternity is built into the universe, which is an amazing thought. Yet, we like to think of a *beginning* of everything.

"...God created..."(v 1)

It is probably just as good to assume that God exists, as that he/she/it doesn't. It is just as difficult to believe that matter has existed eternally, as that God created everything out of nothing - with the attendant question, "Where did God come from?" Whether one has a strictly scientific viewpoint, or a religious one, each view of the universe is as mind-boggling as the other!

"...the Heaven and the Earth."(v 1)

The Heaven was the expanse that the storyteller and the listeners could see above them, but empty of sun, moon, stars and planets (which were not made till Day 4), and full of water. The Earth was flat, and the centre of the universe, naturally, just as our lives are, for each of us, the centre of our world. Heaven, as the place where God resides, must have existed separately from the Heaven created in Genesis, which is translated as "sky" in modern translations, since it obviously meant the dome to keep out imagined water, and the space within, which, later, came to house all the "lights". The Heaven, understood to be God's residence, is evidently outside the firmament.

"And God said..."(v 6)

The most important thing to ask, when someone says "God says...", is "Who says, 'God says'?" It is obvious that no one was alive to hear, whether or not God said anything! Yet, there are always people who claim to know the unknowable, and people gullible enough to suspend their common sense, and believe them.

The Church teaches that the Holy Spirit later told the writers that God said those things. That might even be plausible, if the writers proved to be good, honest, kind and moral. But who were the writers? "Moses", say the Jews, "wrote Genesis, Exodus, Leviticus, Numbers and Deuteronomy - only the record of his death was inserted later". The Church does not take the view that Moses wrote these books, but that Jewish scholars wrote them, much later, and with an exaggerated and idealised view of the characters and events described. How exaggerated and idealised, we will try to gauge later. Egyptian religious beliefs and practice influenced the laws and rituals, instituted by Moses, and Babylonian myths, assimilated during the Exile (586-539 BC), became part of Jewish sacred literature, and thus were included in their canon of scripture, drawn up around 100 AD.

We all love stories, but they do not have to be factual to be worth listening to: they can be fictional and have a lot to teach. It is not just history and science that we can learn from, or be edified by, or enjoy.

The creation story of Genesis 1 makes and apt prologue to the Bible, making the point, that the universe did not just happen - God created it We do not have to look for any deeper meaning than that, and certainly *not* try to believe, or teach, that it is *literally true*. Here is a summary:

On Day 1, after the creation of Heaven and a watery, chaotic Earth, *light* was created, called *day* (without the sun), and separated from darkness, called *night*. The very *names* were given by God, we are told, in all the languages that the Bible would be translated into - if verse 5 is to make any sense to a reader.

On Day 2, a dome is created in the sky, to hold back the water, which would otherwise flood the Earth. This dome, called "firmament" in the Authorised Version, is given the name "heaven", forgetting that Heaven has already been created on, or before, Day 1!

On Day 3, land and sea are separated, with all kinds of plant life.

On Day 4, the sun, moon, planets and stars are placed inside the dome.

On Day 5, sea creatures and birds are created.

On Day 6, the rest of the animal kingdom is created, including human beings, both male and female.

On Day 7, God took a rest. This is so cute! How can *God* get tired?

To take such stories literally is to create all sorts of problems of understanding, and even to undermine the main message of the stories. For example, if the main message of Genesis 1 is that God made everything, this can be quite happily assented to by educated, thinking people, who also believe what science has to teach about a Big Bang and evolution. But if they are told they must take the stories literally, then the main message becomes obscured in wrangles over the six day creation, plants growing on Earth before the sun was created, and such like. Insisting on a literal interpretation, brings the stories into disrepute, because that is intellectually untenable. The established churches know this, and no longer insist on a literal interpretation of the early Genesis stories (Chapters 1-11), which scholars tell us are ancient myths, told over thousands of years of oral tradition, before they were ever written down.

We all wonder how the universe came into being, and many scientists are engaged in trying to probe this mystery. They push the frontiers of knowledge further and further into the past, yet they do not say definitively, "This is the answer." They tell us of a Big Bang, but they admit they do not know the cause of it. Religious people are sometimes not so humble, and it would become them to be so. Instead, without any reason, except that it is written in a book they call "holy" - which only means "set apart for special use" - many of them claim to have the answers to "life, the universe and everything".

Stories are bound to arise when people are confronted with mystery. Some will be attempts to explain it. Some may attempt to deepen it, from various motives. The creation stories in Genesis (for there are two) were, doubtless, composed to answer the wonder felt by primitive people, as they looked at the world around them, and contemplated the rising and setting of the sun every day. "Where does it go every night? How does it get across to the other side, to rise there in the morning? Who lights those little lights in the sky every night?" There were more questions than these: "Why do we suffer pain? Why do some plants have thorns that tear our skin? Why do weeds grow so well? Why do snakes have no legs?" There is always someone who "knows" the answer. This is fine, as long as we know we are only listening to a good *story* - for we all love stories, as I have said - but it is *not* so fine, when the story-teller insists that we must believe his version of events, or else we will go to hell! *Then*, it becomes a power tool, a means of *controlling* others. This is the sinister side of religion, which fundamentalists, cults and authoritarian religions revel in. Beware of it, and of them! Whoever subscribes to an authoritarian religion gives others a rod to beat him (or her) with.

As primitive people sat round their campfires, after their evening meal, there were a few hours to fill in before bedtime, in lands where the sun sets fairly near to six in the evening, with nearly twelve hours of darkness. The storyteller would be a popular member of the group, if he could spin a good yarn, holding the attention of the others. Some stories would become favourites, and be requested often, and the listeners would learn to join in when there was repetition, like the audience at our pantomimes. "Tell us the one about how the world began", they might ask. They could join in, "and it was so", "And the evening and the morning were the (first, second...) day".

"In the beginning God created the heaven and the earth", we read in Genesis 1, verse 1. We usually think of "the heaven" as the place where the sun, moon, planets and stars are - but, no, they are not created until Day 4 of this account of the creation of the universe in six days. There is no harm in these stories as *stories*. They show that primitive people, who did not have formal education, were, nevertheless, intelligent and reflective. The stories of the first eleven chapters of Genesis were passed down the generations, and passed around the various nations and tribes for thousands of years, before they were collected and put into the Bible. And much more sensible they were than some of the stories we teach our children today, however quaint we might find "Goldilocks" or "Jack and the Beanstalk" - at least we tell them, and hear them, as fiction. The trouble comes when pushy people tell fiction as *fact,* and as history.

Some Christians like to see the Six-Day Creation Story as compatible with evolution, interpreting each day as an eon, a long period of evolution. They even interpret "Let there be light" as the flash of the Big Bang, with the other days, also, representing millions of actual years, with man and other mammals marking the latest stage in evolution. The trouble with this interpretation is that plants are growing before the sun is in the sky. No, it does not fit with that interpretation. The best way to see the story of Creation is as an assertion that God is alive, and in control of the universe. It should *not* be taken as an account of *how* or when the universe came into being. After all, the storyteller was only a human being, like his listeners. He was *not* present with God, watching the Creation, listening to the words, knowing God's mind.

In fact, people do wonder whether the universe happened all by itself, or whether it was all instigated by God - accident or design. There are three alternatives, as I see it.

The first is to accept eternity as built-in to the universe, and understand that matter always was, and always will be in existence in some form or another, and that the universe came about when a change occurred in already existing substance. If there was a Big Bang, it certainly must have been *mindbogglingly* big, judging by the size scientists tell us the universe is, but it had a *cause in nature.*

The second explanation is that of the New Physics, which thinks there could be a Higher Intelligence behind the universe, which set everything in motion and remains "out there", watching. Those who have proposed this idea stress that this "Intelligence", is not like the Christian idea of a God, who is interested in us. The God of the New Physics is not at all interested in people as individuals, but only remotely, as a life form on a tiny planet. Not many scientists seem to ascribe to this theory.

The alternative to these two interesting, and even plausible, but comfortless, theories is belief in a Creator who cares. This seems like an impossible belief to many, perplexed by the many problems, mysteries and vexations of life, yet it can bear some serious consideration.

Points to consider are that neither of the first two theories mentioned above gives an explanation for the origins of *life*, as opposed to the origins of the *universe*. Yet, it would seem that the vast universe could quite easily exist without any life forms whatsoever. The second theory attributes life forms to a cold intelligence, which seems to have the ability to design an ear, without any delight in music, poetry or finer feelings. This master-designer can create a world of breath-taking beauty, but takes no pleasure in it. Such a designer is unconvincing. Furthermore, the universe is so vast and full of mystery, that belief in a Creator God, who is interested in us, is not really any more difficult than coping with the mystery of the eternity of matter, or the vastness of the universe, or the size of the Big Bang. The one belief is as difficult as the other! What is *much* more difficult to believe is that the brain just came about accidentally, and that eyesight, hearing, taste, touch or smell just developed by themselves. I find that impossible to believe. The very five senses convince me of a designer, of God.

"Let us make man in our image."(v 26)

Surely it is man's arrogance that makes him think he is made in God's image! It certainly does not flatter God, for people who embrace that creed are often amongst the most obnoxious, and certainly amongst the most ruthless. But, then, so is the God depicted in Genesis: he is a *monster*! Not that his character is revealed in Chapter 1. There, the picture is of an all-powerful but remote Creator, assumed to be *good*, since this is the verdict of satisfaction, pronounced at each stage of creation. Creation, as well as the objects created, are good, so God is "good". He is certainly not shown as *loving*, and very soon he is shown as *hating*, except that the hating is called "righteousness", as we will see in Chapters 2 and 3.

The person who takes the phrase "in God's image" as part of his creed, all too often goes on to think that he, then, is superior to those who do not subscribe to such a belief. Church leaders still love to claim the moral high ground in society, and regularly make public pronouncements on all kinds of topics. They seem to be without any sense of irony or shame, that their "Holy Book" features horrifying crimes against humanity, committed by both God and by his "Holy Nation", or that the conduct of the churches, as institutions, as well as that of many clerics, both long ago and at the present time, leave much to be desired.

One of the saddest aspects of religion is that, very often, the religious person is arrogant and intolerant of others. Is that "in God's image"? It cannot be, for it certainly puts ordinary people off religion, and rightly so! Thousands of sermons have been preached on the words, "made in God's image", insisting that all possible virtues that human beings can possess, stem from this, ignoring the nasty character God is shown to have, as early as Chapter 2, and ignoring also the sins and crimes of so-called godly people throughout history. The composer of the story probably only meant that God looked human, not to frighten his audience. Chapter 1 does not say, even, that God is male, since "Adam" means "mankind", and verse 27 says "male and female".

"... have dominion over the fish of the sea, and over the fowl of the air, and over the cattle, and over all the earth, and over every creeping thing..."   (v 26)

This is the verse, reiterated in Ch 9, at the end of the Noah story, that has given an easy conscience to many people who have misused and abused animals, who have plundered the Earth's resources, poisoning it and spoiling it, and thought they had every right to do so. Many obviously still think this way, cutting down or burning rainforests, ruining the rightful places of abode of tribal people, who have lived in harmony with nature for thousands of years, and the rightful habitats of animals, birds and insects that need those irreplaceable sanctuaries.

Exploit, use, seize, plunder, despoil, rob, kill, have no mercy, get rich quick! All of these actions follow logically from the licence given in the words, "have dominion over", repeated in verse 28, along with "subdue the Earth".

Religions have led the way in cruelty to animals, practising animal sacrifice, in order to let human beings off the hook for sins of omission or commission, or just to placate an evil-intentioned god or spirit. The religion of the Old Testament is largely based on animal sacrifice, which was quite normal for ancient religions. From a human being's point of view, this was, at least, better than *human* sacrifice, in case, one day, *you* became the sacrifice - as happened to some unfortunate Hebrew children (Judges 11 v 31; 2 Kings 16 v 3). Human sacrifice was perfect to practise on an enemy - for it was a neat way of getting rid of those whose territory, or cattle, indeed *all* of whose possessions you wanted - and this is the other main aspect of Old Testament religion! If you regard human beings, whose Land you want, as lower than animals, then it is only a step, into sacrificing them, also, to your own, invented, territorial and bloodthirsty God. *This* is the case with Old Testament religion.

Justifying the unjustifiable from religion, animal abuse went on unchecked down the centuries. Overworked and underfed beasts of burden; wild animals cruelly tamed, in order to break their wills, and perform, for people's amusement; cocks and dogs made to fight to the death, for entertainment; zoos, which neglected the needs of their exhibits, and drove them mad in small and uninteresting cages; these examples are only the tip of the iceberg, in the mass of suffering caused through a widespread attitude that people should be allowed to do what they like, to animals they own. This attitude to animals, is condoned in the Old Testament. "Animals do not have a soul," Church leaders taught, seeking to justify their callousness. Only with the rise of atheism has a better attitude arisen in the West, with compassion for animals, to the *shame of religion*.

The same disrespect towards the Earth's wildlife, down the generations, has caused the needless loss of many species, through deliberate slaughter, through sheer disregard of their needs, through failure to value them, and through destruction of habitats. It is only in the modern climate of healthy questioning of religious dogma, that a kinder approach to the care of animal and plant life, indeed of the planet itself, has arisen in Western society. Societies which lived in harmony with nature - tribal peoples all over the world - were, all too often, despised by Christian explorers and settlers, whose only concern was to amass wealth, by way of taking their lands, their minerals their very means of survival. Nor was the condescending attitude of many missionaries much better. But then, this was the attitude, and that was the behaviour, spelled out in their holy book, the Bible,as a godly way to behave!

If the Earth's plant life has fared better than its animal life, at the hands of the Christian West, it is only by default. The manic researching to make seeds that yield more for less, mass-producing them, and sowing them everywhere, discarding less promising seeds - all this has brought unforeseen hazards. Crops without resistance to certain diseases and pests, coupled with the depletion of the gene banks, are now causing scientists great concern. Fortunately, there are far-seeing people working to save as many of the wild species of plants as they can for future generations, who may one day desperately need variety, in order to grow plants with different properties, adaptability, or resistance to disease or other attack. However, genetic modification of plants is causing great alarm to thinking people because of the possible grave, unforeseen consequences of interfering with nature at such a basic level - "juggling with the building blocks of life".

Many Native Americans, who lived off huge buffalo herds, treating them with great respect, and killing only what they needed, and no more, however plentiful they were, apologised to each animal they killed, and thanked it when they ate it *in order to live*. Yet they were regarded as uncivilised by those who came from Europe with guns, and shot buffalo *for fun*, or for spite, or, worst of all, as a strategy to starve the native people to death, and take their lands. Those were the people whose religion came from a book, and they were living by it, subduing the Earth!

Scotland's great poet, Robert Burns, displays an attitude akin to those Native Americans of the plains, in his poem, TO A MOUSE (on turning up her nest with the plough, November 1785). Echoing the words of the Authorised Version of the Bible, he laments man's lording it over the animal world, and hints at a more humane attitude towards animals, which would bring better treatment:

> I'm truly sorry man's dominion
> Has broken nature's social union,
> And justifies that ill opinion
> Which makes thee startle
> At me, thy poor, Earth-born companion
> And fellow mortal.

"Be fruitful and multiply, and replenish the Earth, and subdue it..." (v 28)

In the last decade of the 20th century many churchmen have claimed that "the Bible is green". Indeed, several years ago, the National Bible Society of Scotland held a competition for schoolchildren with this very title. But *claiming* it is so does not make it so, and it *is* not so. The Bible is ecologically unsound. From the plundering of the famous cedars of Lebanon for David's palace and Solomon's Temple in Jerusalem, to the misapplication in this modern era of the injunction in verse 28, "Be fruitful and multiply" - some religious authorities, or individuals taking a stance against birth control - religion has given a fearful example to the world of self-interest, dogmatism, and lack of foresight. Unlimited human population is the surest and quickest way to destroy the Earth, and is in total contradiction to a belief in its creation by a good and loving God.

It is the ultimate self-denouncement when a religion says that it will not sanction birth control *even for the good of the planet*. If the planet was made by God, and is the gift from God of a beautiful home, with sustainable life for our children, it should be seen as the biggest *treasure*, that we *must* not spoil, and that we ought to look after *very* carefully, in order to pass it on as unspoilt as possible. We should not abuse it by overpopulation.

The injunction to "be fruitful and multiply", sounds like a good idea - if given to a small population with huge territory to fill. This was, presumably, the case in the Genesis 1 story, where the recommendation was given. The words were not spoken to Adam and Eve, who are two characters in a *different* creation story, which starts at Genesis 2 v 4. In Chapter 1, we read that human beings, both male and female, were created, with the *recommendation* - it does not *have* to be a *command* - to "be fruitful and multiply". Nor does it have to mean, even to Fundamentalists, that they have as many children as possible, or do not practise birth control: to have one or two children is still to multiply! Common sense tells us that, since the Earth is finite, even if it is sensible and desirable to increase world population at the time when numbers are small, there *must* come a time to stop doing so. We are *bound* to run out of space, for we all need space, and, the higher our standard of living - and everyone aspires to a higher standard of living - the more space we need, and want. Not only do huge populations put pressure on land for space to live and move about on, we outstrip its capacity to feed its inhabitants. Hence the controversial moves at present into genetically modified food. There are too many people on the planet, and we are *ruining* it thereby. There must be an optimum of food production, and, even more seriously, of *water* availability for consumption. Nor does this take account of the problem of *waste* disposal of large populations of human beings.

It seems a pity to have children as a religious *duty*, and not out of sheer love for them, or for the partner chosen as the other parent. But, then, some religious people like to attribute *everything* they do to God. Even when most of us would say we just *fancied* having a new suit, or such, they will say that it was God s will, for they have to look tidy in the Lord's service - which may be true enough.

The trouble is that some people, with *silly* religious ideas, take "Be fruitful and multiply" as a *command* from God to *all* people for *all* time. The same words are reiterated to Noah in 9 v 1. To increase in numbers, sensible for a time, is *not* sensible forever; it is manifestly crazy, and is the reason I call such religious ideas "silly". They are silly because they fly in the face of all logic and sound reasoning. Obviously the world, is bound to become full up from the implementing of that policy, and therefore, in the name of common sense, it has to stop! Children at primary school can see that. So do sensible religious people.

The Population Explosion - the multiplying of the number of human beings on the planet to *enormous* numbers - is a terrifying prospect. Already large numbers of the world's people live wretched lives of near starvation and hard work, forced to live in totally unsuitable places, trying to scratch a living in desert areas that should not be populated at all. Unchecked human numbers mean the extinction, and near-extinction, of thousands of species of wildlife, as we destroy their habitats, and even of the few remaining animals themselves, for frivolous purposes - for example, the ivory trade, or (so-claimed) aphrodisiacs.

Now that it is possible to curtail human numbers by various methods of contraception, it becomes possible to provide a more comfortable and healthier life for all - but only if we keep numbers down. Each can have a bigger share of the collective cake. It also becomes possible to give a better life to animals, by admitting that they have a right to a place on the planet, and by retreating from their habitats, in order to allow more of them to thrive. After all, they were all on the planet before we were.

Another undesirable aspect of taking the "Be fruitful and multiply" words as a religious duty, is that women, instead of being *people*, equal in status to men, able to make choices as to how they live their lives, are in danger of becoming baby factories, overworked, with their health undermined, as well as that of their children. In societies where having large numbers of children is the culture, it keeps families poor, nations poor, and brings about the exploitation of children. We see this all over the developing world. Where families are large, the parents cannot afford to feed them all. Instead of going to school, or being allowed to play, they have to *work*. Children, looking as young as four, weave in and out of dangerous traffic, trying to sell things. The children are virtual slaves, suffering all sorts of cruel exploitation, sometimes even molestation. Children should *not* have to endure that. They should be loved and looked after, *not* be responsible for looking after their parents or siblings, *nor* sent out to fend for themselves. That means we need to limit the numbers of them that we have.

When populations become oversized, they need more territory. That usually means going to war with their neighbours, who may also be in need of more land. Going to war is wicked, and wanting the land of your neighbours is greedy. They have the right to theirs, just as you have the right to yours! When the land becomes fought over, the young become *cannonfodder*. This is *not* the kind of adulthood the 21st century should be offering its young! Each nation needs to address itself to the matter of numbers, and act responsibly, according to the numbers its land can *sustain*. Leaders should be looking to the quality of life of their subjects, working out policies for the welfare of all, instead of keeping a *few* rich, and *many* in abject misery, with those who can escape, getting out.

Religion has traditionally been used for the *control* and *manipulation* of people, and some branches of the Church still intrude very much into the personal lives of their members, particularly in the matter of birth control. In some countries, the Roman Catholic Church has power to prevent family planning from being offered even to married couples. This is *abuse of power*, and brings, ironically, in its wake, *demands for abortion* which could be avoided if *contraception* was not denied to couples wishing to use it. In many developing countries, abortion is used as birth control, because contraception is denied people, and, although abortion is also prohibited, desperate people resort to dangerous, desperate measures in an effort to have some control over their lives.

Any intelligent and moral person sets a limit on his/her procreating, *in order to be fair to everyone else*. To have more than a few children is selfish, for *everyone* needs a space in the world. Someone said to me, "People should have as many children as they can afford". I say, "No! For the rich to have more is unfair. Rich and poor should have equal rights in this, as in *everything*. A few children should be the norm for everyone."

It is also *cruel* to children, to have many. At *family* level, parents can only cope adequately with a few. When the few become many, what often happens is that the older children are lumbered with looking after their siblings. This is *not fair* either to the older or the younger children, who deserve to have *parents* looking after them. At *national* level, it is dangrous to the children, for a country's leaders may view them as a *potential army*, and send them off to war. As a veteran of the First World War said about it in a TV programme recently, "Life was cheap. Human beings should be *valued*". Large families, in the early part of the century, made war too easy an option for politicians, who viewed the large populations of young men as expendable. (They themselves would be safe!) Parents in Europe might not so easily have accepted declarations of war, if they had had only one or two sons, instead of five or six! They might have argued with their leaders, and insisted on peaceful negotiations, instead of war. The assassination of the Archduke Franz Ferdinand, which is given as one of the main reasons for the outbreak of the First World War, was not a *reason* it was only an *excuse*. The war must have been desired by politicians. Franz Ferdinand was *nothing* to the men, who went off to fight. They must have wondered every day in the trenches what on Earth they were doing there, and why they were sacrificing their lives! Large families give an excuse for war. They are cannonfodder!

"Be fruitful and multiply, and replenish the Earth"? It is already overpopulated. It is being damaged, poisoned and overused, as though our planet home were a thing of no consequence, instead of our most precious possession! We should love it, respect it, cherish it, care for it. Not to care about the preservation of the Earth is not to love our children, or any future generation. It is also not to care for the rest of creation. Not to love and care for the planet, in all its amazing diversity, is not to love God, either. To overpopulate the Earth is to be very immoral!

"...and it was very good."
(v 31)

The authors of the ancient myths of Genesis 1 - 11, like countless religious people throughout the ages, claimed to know the mind of God. How is it, then, that the world is still in the tragic state of nation at war with nation, and even within nations, with much, if not most, of the trouble caused by people who claimed to know the mind of God? Others might be led to infer from that, that God has caused a lot of the trouble. But it is too easy to blame God. We need to look to *ourselves*!

"Good" is the verdict pronounced on everything created from Day 3 to Day 5. On Day 6, it is even "very good" - so good, in fact, that, by the next chapter, God is making death threats on the poor souls, who did not ask to be created, and, in Chapter 3, he is inflicting harsh punishments for a trumped-up sin, certainly no *crime*, whilst before Chapter 9, he has drowned everything and everyone, save a few! "Good" in the Bible cannot be what we ordinarily mean by "good", especially when we discover, very soon after this, that many of the greatest heroes of the book are murderers, thugs and genocidal maniacs - as we shall see.

Or - is the reason why the rest of the Bible, and many Bible-based religions are so violent, that, as early as Chapter 2, the Creator God who made all things "good", has been replaced by a wicked *imposter*, bent on doling out harsh punishments for nothing and next-to-nothing, on everything and everyone, upon the least pretext? It seems like it. There is a shock in Chapter 2 - for the God who, in Chapter 1, we assumed was well-disposed towards his creation, suddenly reveals himself to be different from what we expected. Is Chapter 2 a homing-in on the God of Chapter 1, or does Chapter 2 replace the God of Chapter 1 with another? Whichever the explanation is, *there is something far wrong with the picture of God emerging as early as Chapter 2*!

We need to think about that.

CHAPTER 6

ADAM AND EVE: GENESIS 2 & 3

The Church teaches that, in this story, God is good, loves his creation, and wants to nurture a people of faith, people who are morally good, and enjoy their fellowship eternally. This is to *make* the story say what ministers, or teachers *want* it to say, but really, it is *not* a story about morality, or faith. It is about *blind obedience* to a dictator. Although the Church no longer teaches this story as literally true, calling it "The Fall of Man", saying sin entered the world when Adam (why not Eve?) ate the fruit of the forbidden tree, yet it *still* teaches it as a valid picture of God's relationship with humankind. Adam's sin (although he never existed), not our own, is still presented as the reason we need a saviour, for the *whole creation* is under condemnation because of what mythical Adam did! Christ is still presented as "the second Adam, who came to our rescue" - each person individually - and to redeem the whole of creation, which is, supposedly, ruled by the Devil, sometimes called Satan, or "the God of this world" (as in 2 Corinthians 4 v 4, and 1 John 5 v 19)!

But blind obedience is *not* faith, and *blind obedience* is what this tyrannical and vindictive monster of a God will have! Adam and Eve, in the Garden of Eden, are invited to eat the fruit of any tree, except one, in the middle of the garden, the Tree of the Knowledge of Good and Evil. No loving explanation is given to the couple, of the danger they run, if they *do* eat, as a parent would give, in warning a child of danger. On the contrary, there is something chilling in the loveless tone of, "Thou shalt not eat of it; for in the day that thou eatest thereof thou shalt surely die" (2 v 17). It sounds as though he *knew* they would eat the fruit, and was rubbing his hands in glee, at the thought of punishing the pair! Of course they would eat it; it was only a matter of time! In fact, by banning it in the way he did, without explaining thoroughly the consequences, he was *inviting* them to eat it! What a sly God this is! How devious!

Yet the *snake* gets the blame for being cunning! How convenient to blame the snake! But it will not do! God has just created the snake in Chapter 1, and it was *good*. And so comes the perennial problem of, "Where did evil come from?" We should *not* accept meekly the Church's traditional explanation, that this was Satan in the guise of a snake, or, again, that Satan was making use of the natural badness of the snake. Not only is this unfair to snakes, it goes against the pronouncement of "good" upon the creation! No! This is the Church reading into the story what is not there, blindly accepting the interpretation of the story in Revelation 12 v 9, "the great dragon was cast out, that old serpent, called

24

the Devil and Satan This is part of the *angelology* folklore, referred to here and there in the Bible, where Satan is an angel, along with Michael, Gabriel, and other "sons of God" (Gen. 6 v 4).

In fact, there are very few references to Satan in the Old Testament, although it is a book full of the most heinous acts - but they are called *righteous*! He makes his first appearance in 1 Chronicles 21 v 1, where he is in David's head, prompting him to take a census. Why *this* should be a wicked thing, when *genocide* was *not* wicked is a question that should engage the minds of Christian scholars. However, they are more interested in the academic question of why two censuses were all right *before* (Numbers 1 and 26), under *Moses*, and why it was said to be *all wrong*, when *David* took one. Who cares? In all three cases, the purpose was primarily to establish the size of the Israelite *army*.

Satan makes his next appearance amongst the angels in Heaven in the book of Job, an ancient folk tale about the problem of suffering. God provokes an argument with Satan over Job's great faith. God is proud of his religious devotion, whereby he continually makes sacrifices for *possible* sins that his children *might* commit. Most of us would think this is going overboard with our religion, but, it seems that *this* is the excessive zeal that God desires of his people! Thereafter, proud God gives Satan permission to test and trouble, undeservedly, poor old Job - simply because God boasted! But good old Job comes through, triumphant, in the end.

To say the *snake* in the Garden of Eden in Genesis is *Satan* is to take the story out of its context, and apply the angelology system learned from later references. To read the story *in* context, as a sequel to Chapter 1, or as a story in its own right, shows up something very different, and more *subtle* and *alarming*. The snake had just been created in Chapter 1, and pronounced to be *good*. There is *no* Satan in the story from start to finish. The *God* in this story is the source of the trouble! This God is the problem.

Which of the characters, God or the snake, tells the truth? It is the snake. God tells a lie! Here begins the *confusion* in Christian theology: the lying God is not recognised for what he is, nor are so many of the rest of the lies, nor evil characters recognised. If the Church has confused *good* with *evil*, that is the biggest of all confusions! It must wake up to this, face up to it, and rethink its understanding of its Holy Book!

The Adam and Eve story shows *the very antithesis of a moral God*, for, far from wishing moral action, he tries, through his lies and threats, to prevent his

25

creatures from being able to exercise any moral choice. Then he is furious with the *snake, who makes moral choice possible* for the two people. *No* moral action is possible without a realistic choice between good and evil, right and wrong. God was furious, but, ironically, the anonymous 15th century writer of a Christmas carol calls the disobedience a *blessing*:

> Blessed be the time
> That apple taken was,
> Therefore we moun singen,
> *Deo gratias*!

Again, at the end of the garden scene, there is a huge discrepancy between what the Church tells us God is like, and how God behaves in this story. After the poor victims of the devious God have been banished from the garden, does he feel like forgiving them, or wish to have anything to do with them in the future? No - he puts a guard on the gate, so that they cannot steal back into the garden, and eat from another tree, the Tree of Life, and live forever. This is in *direct contrast* to what the Church teaches about God being "not willing that any should perish, but that all should come to repentance" (2 Peter 5 v 5). Is any chance given here to the disobedient pair, who are doubtless sorry for their action, to say they are sorry, and be forgiven? (All this pain and suffering for one little fruit! They were *bound* to think it wasn't worth it!) No *hint* of mercy, love or understanding is shown by this hardest of hard-hearted Gods! Why does the Church go on trying to say the two pictures of God are one? They are not.

In any case, the story was composed by a mere mortal like ourselves, and, as such, we can assume the author had no magic hotline to God, especially before human beings were on the planet! Doubtless the story was told in response to the perennial questions that people seemed to ask a few thousand years ago, just as people do now:
Who made this world around us? How did we get here? Who makes the rain? Who put all these lights up there in the sky? Why do we suffer pain? Why do we have to work so hard? Why do weeds grow so well, and not the things we want to?" Well - there is always someone who will come up with an answer! However, we do not have to believe it - and we *should not*, if it does not make sense!

You could be forgiven for wondering whether the writer of Genesis 2, (or even God!) had forgotten so quickly, that he had already created Adam (the Hebrew word for *mankind*) both men and women, in Chapter 1. But no - the reason for this second creation is that it is a separate creation story, from another region, which was collected and set own alongside the other, *as though* it was a continuation of the first tale.

Some Christians do not like to believe this verdict from scholars, preferring to see the Adam and Eve story as a zooming in on a representative pair from those created in Chapter 1 - but this interpretation does not stand up to scrutiny, for the story in Chapter 2 does read as the creation of a single individual, and does not fit with the creation of Eve from his rib. That makes no sense if there are already females in the world, created alongside the males. Fundamentalist Christians seem to ignore the creation of people in Chapter 1, and see the appearance of Adam and Eve in Chapter 2, as the start of the human race. Convenient blindness.

The established churches have had to change their teaching on the stories of the first eleven chapters of Genesis, and, instead of teaching them as factual, and literally true (ignoring the discrepancies), now teach them as symbolic, having lessons to teach but *not* historical, and *not* scientific. The shock to the Church of Darwin's publication, in 1859, of his book, ON THE ORIGIN OF SPECIES, meant that people were no longer prepared to accept blindly the old teaching. Nor can we afford to go on blindly accepting the present day teaching of the Church. We need to keep on thinking, and thinking hard, and *morally*, and *rationally*.

And what about that other trick theologians have up their sleeve for dealing with the embarrassing, ruthless monster of a God depicted in the Old Testament? This is the trick that says that, in the Bible, we are given a *progressive* picture of God. It gets better as we read on through the Bible, they say, until the *full* picture of God comes, in the New Testament, with Jesus. If *that* is what Christian theologians say, *why* do ministers still present the blurred or *bad* pictures, of the murdering God, as *valid*, and the misguided, deluded, massacring heroes of the Old Testament as doing God's will? Their trick is too crude; we see through it. They cannot cope with the dichotomy they find in the Scriptures, except on an academic level. It is now time to deal with it on a moral level.

CHAPTER 7

CAIN AND ABEL: GENESIS 4

This story is propaganda to promote the idea of blood sacrifice. The brothers, Cain and Abel, are, like their parents, Adam and Eve, mythical figures, not historical. They are fictional. No harm in that, as long as they are understood to be such. The trouble is that both the Old and New Testaments treat them as historical, to the confusion of the Church.

Regular churchgoers, like me, have listened to what seems like hundreds of sermons, on a line from this story, "Am I my brother's keeper?" And the answer always comes, at the end of the sermon, "Yes, we are our brother's keeper." No one will quarrel with that; we all should care for others, for "no man is an island", etc, etc.

However, once again, the main thrust of the story is ignored, except by Evangelicals, who are happy to point out the acceptability to God of, nay the *preference* of God for animal sacrifice, as opposed to an offering of vegetables or cereal. "Why?" I ask. "Because he is cantankerous and bloodthirsty", is the only possible answer. But, in reality, this is a distortion of God - the true God would *not* disdain a sincerely offered gift - although, why he requires cereal and vegetables at all, or, even worse, *blood* is not so clear to me! To feed the poor, I hope.

"Our God is gracious", we sing in church. Well, this God is *not* gracious! Preachers of sermons try to justify God's refusal of Cain's offering - although he was first, and obviously brought his gift with great sincerity - from the vague admonition in Ch 4 v 7, "If thou doest well, shalt thou not be accepted?" Evidently *not*, it seems to me - he *did* well, and was not accepted; but that was not his fault - it was just that this God prefers *animal* sacrifice. Cain grew crops, but Abel had *livestock*, and *this* is what the God in *this* religion had his eye on for his adoration. It is inferred that Cain's offering was refused because of some *sin*, and Christian ministers seize on this, in their sermons, to justify God's disdain of Cain's offering. But this is *not* substantiated in the text. Slurs, innuendo and rumour must not be allowed to convict the man. The God is peevish and ungracious at best, bloodthirsty at worst. Read on in the Old Testament - soon *this God himself* is killing whole populations!

After the Tabernacle in the desert and, later, the Temple in Jerusalem were built, the religion of the Hebrews centred round animal sacrifice. Both Tabernacle and Temple were built expressly for that. The story of Cain and Abel was a good one to have in their scriptures to support that style of religion. The prophets eventually became vocal critics of the sacrificial system, and consistently called for a religion based on compassion and justice. They disputed whether the religion of blood sacrifice was valid religion at all. They claimed it was *not*, and that the religion of burning bullocks was utterly abhorrent to God. The 8th century BC prophet Isaiah was particularly stringent about this; "I (God) delight *not* in the blood of bullocks, or of rams, or of he goats" (Isa 1 v 11).

To Cain, it must have seemed there was no pleasing this God, and no reasoning with him, either. Sometimes well-intentioned people are driven to despair. The first murder of the Bible is Cain's slaying of his brother, upset at God, and in a fit of jealousy. How can *anything* go right, when *God* is so wrong? There is another murder in the same chapter (v 23), but no one pays attention to it. The murder of Abel by Cain, two mythical figures, also features quite prominently in the thinking of the New Testament writers. This *mythical* murder is sermonised over and deplored, yet the "murder by wholesale", which forms a *huge* part of the *historical* section of the Old Testament, is ignored. It is also glossed over, in Church sermons, or sometimes weakly lamented, but still inferred to be *necessary*. This is unacceptable.

Cain's punishment for fratricide is banishment from home, and this upsets him again. He is afraid of people, because a stranger is vulnerable, and he is afraid someone will kill him. (Funny how wrongdoers never like other people to do to them what they do!) Fundamentalists think there are no other people alive in the world at this time, so who is Cain afraid of? Of course, there *are* other people! And here is the first sign of a strange mercy in the character of this God. In 4 v 15 God promises to take seven lives for anyone who kills Cain, and puts a protective mark on him! So, the earnest worshipper, whom God was so peevishly against at the beginning of the story, is God's pet, now that he has committed murder, and seven people who have done *nothing*, are under a death threat! *Topsy-turvy values, topsy-turvy Bible!*

Thereupon Cain goes away, to a Land called Nod, and finds a wife there (again, plenty of *people* around) and builds a city. The murderer evidently lives happily ever after, protected by God - as do thousands more murderers in the Bible. We need to ask what this God is about. Is *this* the God that made everything and everyone, or is *this* God an *invention of man*?

29

CHAPTER 8

NOAH AND THE FLOOD: GENESIS 6 - 9

You would not normally think that to drown people and animals proved that you loved them, but in the twisted logic of Christian teaching, this is what you get. And not just in the days when I went to Sunday School! One of the modern hymnaries for children, on sale at present, JUNIOR PRAISE, has a hymn with this ridiculous logic;

> Mister Noah built an ark...
> And only eight were saved...
> Remember God is love.

Also, in 1998, Radio 4 broadcast a Sunday Service from a church in England, the whole theme of which was the Noah story, with the tired old theology that God made everything, all so good, but people became very wicked, and needed to be drowned, so that he could start again (nearly)! Why the *animals* had to be drowned because *people* were wicked was an issue not dealt with. Neither was why tiny babies, who had never done *anything* wrong, had to be drowned. Why a clever God could not have thought of a more selective way of punishing those who were upsetting him so much was similarly ignored, along with why a belief in a Judgment Day, could not have taken care of the matter. The rainbow, at the end of the Flood, is there in the sky, to dazzle the brain, stifle all doubts, and stem all questions. Of course, there was no other way of dealing with some people's *alleged* sins, and the recurrence of rainbows in the sky (sometimes) after rain, clinches any possible argument! *Mass murder by God* is not seen as a sin, not to mention a *crime against humanity!* The first massacre, of the many massacres in the Bible, is perpetrated by *God*. So are most of the others - or so the Bible says!

Harshness, unfairness, over-the-top punishment on God's part - that would have been too mundane a human reaction to feature in *this* church service, where common sense was out of the window. People are *bad*, the story claims, not seeing that the God it is portraying is *worse!*

And anyway, what about God's *sons* coming down from Heaven, and raping beautiful girls, in the verses just *before* the Noah story? (Gen. 6 v 1 - 4) Why isn't *their* sin punished? Oh - that isn't sin? Well, why not? And even more to the point, who *is* this God who punishes like that, and has sons, and doesn't punish them like that? *That is the question!* But asking questions like that is supposed, in some religious circles, to show "a lack of spirituality". And, anyway, there *is* an intellectual answer, which is that by the "sons of God" is meant "angels", who are with God in Heaven, of whose throng Satan used to be one, and Michael and Gabriel are two more. *How anybody knows that* is another question we are not supposed to ask!

And Noah, whom God saved, to father the whole human race again, was *he* a paragon of virtue? - A drunken sot, more like, who curses an innocent grandson for his own debauchery! The alleged crime is that Ham, perhaps quite innocently, discovers his father, in a drunken stupor, naked, and tells his brothers. They are too polite to look, but cover him up. Noah, on hearing what happened, in a rage, utters a curse on Ham's poor, unsuspecting and guiltless son, Canaan, who, as far as the story tells, had nothing whatsoever to do with the affair. But this is often the way with debauched people - they blame the innocent for *their* crimes.

On one level, the Noah story is an answer to the natural question, "Why do floods occur?" There were many stories about floods, great floods, where many people were drowned. "They must be punishment for sin", said the weavers of yarns. Two such stories found their way into the Bible, with two different numbers of animals going into the Ark (Ch 6 v 20 and Ch 7 v 2). At this level, the Noah story ends with the rainbow, the sign of a promise - God will never drown the whole creation again! The fact that he should *not* have done it in the first place is never even suggested!

And, as though the drowning of practically *all* the animals alive, was not *enough* slaughter of them, when Noah at length emerges from the Ark, *he kills another pair of every kind of (clean) animal (8 v 20)* - even more gratutitous slaughter - as a (very *suitable* and acceptable, according to v 21) offering to God! Presumably he allowed them to procreate first, else the newly *saved* animals would have been made *extinct* after all! We noticed in the previous chapter, this God's predisposition to blood sacrifices, and to an absence of logic or any kind of common sense. Although pleased with the sweet smell of the success of all the butchery, still this God remains sour in his attitude to people; "the imagination of man's heart is evil from his youth" (8 v 21). He should apply *this* judgment to himself!

But the story has a deeper level, and very *sinister* it is. At that level, it does *not* end with the rainbow. It ends with the *cursing of Canaan*. And this curse on Canaan, is the real reason for the story being in Hebrew sacred literature, for it gives the Hebrews of future generations an excuse (*not* a reason, but an *excuse*) to despise the Canaanites, and, eventually, to slaughter them - all in the name of God and righteousness!

31

CHAPTER 9

MELCHIZEDEK: GENESIS 14 v 18 - 20

Practically *nothing* is known about this King and Priest of Jerusalem, but this does not deter the writers of the Bible, and later commentators, from saying *plenty.* The author of Psalm 110, accords him an eternal priestly order, superior to that of Aaron, in a verse taken by the Church to be a messianic reference, "Thou art a priest for ever, after the Order of Melchizedek", (also Heb 5 v 6). The epistler to the Hebrews, in Chapter 7, goes to town on Melchizedek, making great play of his having no recorded genealogy, inferring he had no parents, and thus was planted there, in Jerusalem, miraculously, by God, at that time, to symbolise eternity and Christ! This is to make a parallel where there is *no* parallel, for, obviously, Melchizedek had parents. It makes *much* out of *nothing*, inferring *huge* significance of his parentage not being recorded. It would have been surprising if it *had* been recorded: King Abimelech's genealogy is not recorded, nor is the Pharaoh's, with whom Abraham had to do...

The writer of Hebrews also uses Melchizedek's blessing of Abraham, to make the point that Christ's law is superior to the Levitical Law, because the greater blesses the lesser. Thus, he argues, Melchizedek is superior to Abraham, and Christianity to Judaism! If he thinks this is so, why does he support the religion of Abraham, which went on to plan the slaughter of Melchizedek's Jebusite people, ending his line, and his religion (which he has just said are *eternal* and *superior!*) in order to take their Land and their capital city, Jerusalem? It would have been more logical to support *Melchizedek's* religion and people. But logic is not this writer's strong point, just as Christian logic goes haywire, with regard to the Old Testament. Immoral sentiments are attributed to God, and immoral commands, which are contradictory, illogical and senseless - but, much worse, *wicked*!

Abraham's gift to the priest/king of a tenth of the booty he has just won in a small war, becomes the amount promised by Jacob to God if he blesses him (Gen. 28 v 22), and, subsequently the "tithing" that some Christian churches expect from their members. Christian cults even demand a minimum of a tenth of a member's income as proof of their commitment to the cult, and of their love for God. Funny to think that the origin of what is often regarded as proof of one's devotion to God was the dividing up of *plunder*!

There are only three verses in Genesis, telling of Abraham's encounter with Melchizedek. Far from Judaism teaching the world monotheism, in days when the world was full only of idolatrous religions, here was Melchizedek, "priest of *The Most High God* "(Gen. 14 v 18), testimony to a monotheistic religion in the Jebusite capital of Jerusalem! The gracious, priestly King feeds Abraham and his retinue of hundreds, blessing them, as, doubtless, he blessed many others.

It is probably always wise to keep in with an army on one's doorstep, and Melchizedek certainly gave no excuse for it to attack him. Indeed, Abraham's troops were, according to all that we are told, defensive, and only attacked in order to save his nephew, Lot, when he got caught up in a small war and was captured. Nomads were accepted in Canaan, and Abraham seems been accepted as such, and welcomed. But, although his 318 trained, fighting men did not go around attacking, they did, no doubt, command respect.

However, Abraham was *not* a true nomad; he was spying out the Land, eyeing up what land he wanted for a certain line of his descendants to possess exclusively, and settle on. Did Melchizedek fail to realise this? We cannot know. What is certain is that Abraham was always able to fool people, and Melchizedek, who symbolises peace and righteousness, seems not to have suspected the guile of his guest, who passed on his dream of having, not just the *city* of Jerusalem, but the whole *Land* - one day. The peaceful priest could not have guessed that this Abraham, with his despicable offering from the spoils of war, would bequeath on Jerusalem a fearful future.

Ironically, Heb 7 v 2 stresses that Melchizedek represents righteousness and peace, neither of which virtues were in the hearts of Abraham, who paid tribute to him, nor David, who is credited with writing about him in the Psalm. The *blessings* were remembered, but *peace* and *righteousness* were ignored as the way to live. The words were good for paying lip-service to, but *deceit* and war were ever Abraham's and David's ways of living.

An even bigger irony is this: to say that Melchizedek's priesthood was greater than the (later) Aaronic priesthood, and to align Christ's priesthood with Melchizedek's, not Aaron's, is to bypass the religion of Judaism completely, and link it with *the Canaanite religion* of the Jebusites of an era before Abraham - and this point is made by a Jewish writer!

Yet, *missing his own point completely*, a few chapters later (11), this same author of the Letter to the Hebrews lists the destroyers of all that Melchizedek stood for, and calls them heroes of the faith! Heroes of Judaism they may be, but heroes of Christianity they cannot be. The prophet Amos, aware of something *very* wrong in the religion, said, in Chapter 5 v 26 of his prophecy, that the objects of their sacrifices were *idols*, Moloch and Chiun. He was also aware of the lack of moral content in the religion: justice was missing, and *justice* was what God wanted, he said. It must be so.

Thus the Jewish author of Hebrews even missed the significance of the most significant point he made, and that is - Jesus is *outwith* Judaism, transcending it! It is high time for Christianity to latch on to this point, too.

CHAPTER 10

THE OLD COVENANT; GENESIS 12 - 25

"This is my blood of the New Covenant, shed for many, for the remission of sins." (Matthew 26 v 28)

Christianity sees the New Covenant in Christ as depending on the validity of the Old. Thus Christianity has traditionally taught the Chosen People and the Promised Land, taking Abraham's claims at face value. He claims to have God's directing when he sets out from home, in search of another place to live. He soon finds it (v 7) - easily recognisable, for it is a fertile land, "A Land Flowing with Milk and Honey". It is Canaan. He does not tell the Canaanites he intends to have their Land, but he tells his heirs, when they come along, that God has made a Covenant with him, to bless him, and give him many descendants (v 2), and the Land of Canaan.

This Covenant is the climax of the dream, which dominates Abraham's life, so that everything he does is in pursuit of it. But the dream, so sweet to him, would *not* have been so sweet to his unsuspecting hosts. Whilst they shower him with gifts, and want to make a present of the field with trees and cave, which he wants to buy to bury Sara in, they offer it to him for *nothing*, for sheer *friendship*. Little do these generous Hittites know that already, in Abraham's conversations with God, they have become the "enemy" (22 v 17), to be supplanted in future *wars*, that the incomer's descendants will wage against theirs. Little do they know his *dream* will become their *nightmare* and little do they know his "Shalom" does *not* mean "peace!"

Traditional Christian teaching takes Abraham's part, and, since Jesus accepted him as God's man, it, likewise, presents him as God's man. But apply Liberation Theology to the Bible, and a very *different* interpretation from the traditional teaching comes across. God would *not* secretly collude with an ambitious and determined man to give *any* of his descendants the right to kill off millions of people still unborn! It is the height of gullibility to believe anyone who would *make* such a claim. If God is *God*, he *must* love everyone equally, *not* single any out for special blessings, and *certainly not* turn them into terrorists and murderers! If God is *not* like this, then he is not worth worshipping!

Let Abraham's *actions* reveal his character. Apart from the strange goings-on with Sara, his first wife, marrying her off to other men, how does he treat the others? First of all, he allows Sara to treat Hagar, his concubine (Sara's *gift*, since she wanted her slave to have a surrogate child for her) so cruelly, that the poor girl runs away. Eventually, after Sara has her own son, and no longer needs the surrogate one, she prevails upon Abraham to send her away. For all they care, both mother and son could die in the desert. This is unforgivable on both Abraham's and Sara's parts.

There were other wives, after Sara, one of whom was called Keturah (25 v 1). *All* the children (although daughters are not specifically mentioned) are sent away, albeit with gifts, from Isaac (v 6), the favoured one. *No* parent has the right to treat his children so badly and so unfairly. Such treatment should not be condoned, far *less* be attributed to *God*!

Is it his guilty conscience, or is it mental illness that inspire the next scene? I do *not* accept it as God-inspired. He takes Isaac up to a mountain, where he believes God has told him to sacrifice him. They set the fire for burning the offering, and Isaac is tied up, and placed on the altar, ready to be killed and burnt (22 v 9). Then the father picks up knife to kill the child, believing God was demanding this. Luckily for Isaac, the father heard another voice, just in time. It told him *not* to hurt the boy; God was just testing him! A ram was caught by its horns in a thicket nearby. Instead of kindly freeing it and letting it go, as one of God's dumb creatures in difficulty might have expected from one of the "crown of the creation", this poor creature received short shrift, for *it* was summarily executed, and offered up to the deity.

Lots of claims are made about God, and we cannot believe them all! Of *this* claim, there is something important to say, and it is this - if God *inspires* a thought and an action, both the thought and the action must be right and good. If the *thought* is right, then the *action* is also right. But human sacrifice can *never* be right, either in thought or action, therefore *the thought was not of God*! Luckily, the voices Abraham's head, which had inspired the action, also stopped it.

The Church does not see this. Because the story *says* that this was God testing Abraham, the Church believes it! It does not apply moral standards to it. Church members are regaled with readings, sermons and hymns praising Abraham and his God. But Abraham's God champions covetous greed, duplicity, ingratitude, and deception. *This is not God*. This is mental aberration. The Church must address the problem of Abraham's God who inspires poor morality, crazy religion, family neglect, theft of land, and human sacrifice for *testing* purposes!

CHAPTER 11

JACOB AND ESAU; GENESIS 25 - 33

The names "Abraham, Isaac and Jacob", grandfather, father and son recur constantly throughout the Old Testament, to identify the God with whom later leaders of the nation were in touch. Moses and the prophets reassured the population that the God they spoke for was "the God of Abraham, Isaac and Jacob", and that what they were saying was in tune with the promises made to the patriarchs. But there were other sons, who were passed over for blessing, in a very peculiar way. This is supposed to be due to "the inscrutability of God". I suspect it has more to do with the strange religious ideas of the parents. Certainly, the *character* of the person seems to have nothing to do with God's favour, and that seems arbitrary in the extreme.

Isaac is famous for his birth to a mother, Sara, long past the menopause, after being foretold by two strange visitors, interpreted as being *angels* (the word means "messengers from God") appearing in human form. His wife, Rebecca, who was also his cousin, produced twins (again, a miraculous birth, after a prayer by her husband) Jacob and Esau. They became renowned for their quarrel over which of them should be the greater. *God* had said that the elder would serve the younger (25 v 23), which was the opposite way round from the norm, where the culture conferred important rights of inheritance on the firstborn Whether Rebecca told her younger son of this prediction, thus spurring events, we do not know. What we do know is that Jacob coveted Esau 's privileged position as head of the siblings - for there were others (27 v 29) - thus revealing a very unlovely streak in his character. He took steps to procure Esau's rights.

Of course the teller of the tale, and, even more so, the compiler of a collection of ancient tales, has always the useful gift of hindsight, and can update the stories with convenient, or significant, inserts. This story begins with the prediction that the younger twin would become the pre-eminent one, religiously speaking. Esau, in the Scripture, seems to be despised even before birth, which has *got* to be unfair, *and* Jacob's cheating character goes uncriticised. God's man could obviously cheat to get his way if he wanted to; that *must* be all right! Strange God!

Jacob was determined to have Esau's inheritance. One might have thought that *brotherly love* would prompt Jacob to run to his starving twin with a plate of lentils he had cooked. Not so! This was the opportunity Jacob had been waiting for, and he seized it. "I'll give you the lentils if you give me your birthright."

"What use is my birthright to me, if I am dead? All right." Far from deploring Jacob's unnatural, calculating action, the Bible slates Esau: "Thus Esau despised his birthright" (25 v 34). This is not *my* assessment of the story. We should notice that the heroes of the Old Testament are people who want to be *great*, but not to be *good*.

Rebecca is given the blame for the next act of treachery, in which Jacob is given the father's deathbed blessing. He meant it for Esau, but Rebecca persuades Jacob to cheat Isaac into believing he is Esau. She prepares the meal he wanted, and covers Jacob's hands and neck with animal skin, in response to the famous line, "Behold, Esau, my brother is a hairy man, and I am a smooth man" (27 v 11)! To give Jacob his due, he is unwilling to cheat his father, fearing it will bring down a curse upon him, if he is found out, rather than a blessing; but Rebecca is willing to risk a curse, and so they deceive the blind old man.

Esau' s tears and wailing tug at the heartstrings, as we read of his dismay on discovering that, once again, his brother has done the dirty on him. He pleads with his father to bless him, too, but, even knowing the treachery, Isaac refuses. Esau has to beg, with more tears, for a paltry, inferior blessing. It would have reflected well on Isaac, if he could have found it in his heart to bestow a blessing of love and kindness on Esau, and even to revoke the blessing on Jacob, making a stand for honesty. Instead, he is hidebound by *tradition*, and by *oracles* claiming to speak for God. Esau says he will kill Jacob, when his father is dead. Rebecca takes charge of this situation, too, and arranges for Jacob to go to Haran, to his uncle's, ostensibly for a wife. He gets yet *another* blessing from Isaac.

At least, Jacob's conscience seems to bother him as he flees from his brother's wrath. At Bethel, on his way north, he has a vivid dream of a ladder reaching up into the sky, with angels going up and down it. This dream is a huge religious experience for Jacob. There, he receives for himself, the promises of multitudes of descendants, and a Land, as his father and grandfather had done. He vows to give God a tenth of his income, if he blesses him. This is a favourite story in Christian sermons and Sunday School lessons.

In Haran, Jacob gets on pretty well, although the cheat gets cheated by his uncle, and, in one week, lands two wives, instead of the one he wanted (29 v 27). He had to work for fourteen years for his uncle, to earn them. He is cheated constantly by his uncle over the following six years, when he is building up some wealth for himself. Jealousies and backbiting make it clear to him that he should move on - back home...

He is a worried man, as he travels south, fearing that Esau might not have forgiven him for what he did to him. He has a restless night before he is due to meet up with his brother, and emerges from another vivid dream with an injured hip, and *a new name*. Look up a dictionary of names, and you will find that "Jacob" means "cheat", as Esau had implied in 27 v 36. However, Jacob deals with that, and in a very religious way, for he comes out of the dream with a much better name, ISRAEL, "God struggles", or, "a prince with God"! Such an imposing name was bound to be cherished, and *this* is the name, *not* Jacob, which his descendants stick to for the rest of the Old Testament and beyond, "The Children of *Israel*".

But Esau has a loving heart, that his self-centred, ambitious brother can never imagine, for all his dreaming! Jacob need not have feared. Although he is willing to bow and scrape to Esau, now, to be forgiven, Esau does not require that. He is the better character. His love is not conditional, like his twin's. He has already forgiven him (33 v 4).

Three cheers for Esau!

CHAPTER 12

JOSEPH, DINAH AND THEIR BROTHERS - GENESIS 34 - 50

Joseph is one of the better characters we find in the Old Testament, which is perhaps the main reason that some of his half-brothers wanted to kill him. He had dreams of being great, and was innocent enough to tell them about them, not realising the fury this caused, even in his father, whose favourite he was, being Rachel's son. (Perhaps he resembled her.) I have often heard Christians - people who should know better than to condone hate - voice the opinion that Joseph deserved the hatred of his brothers. This is shocking! They seemed to think that the wish to do away with Joseph was quite *reasonable*, although telling one's dreams is not *usually* regarded as meriting the death penalty!

He also ran to his father with tales - which did nothing to improve his popularity with the brothers - but, then, there was a lot to tell. They were wild! Some of them, at least, were capable of murder. They planned to leave Joseph to die in a hole. Two of them, Simeon and Levi, later, murdered a whole tribe of Canaanites, treacherously and *irreligiously* (because the males of the Hivite tribe had been circumcised, in a contract with their father - had become, in fact, Israelites).

They gave an excuse for this atrocity, which was that Dinah's husband had slept with her before they were married. "Should he treat our sister like a whore?" (34 v 31) The Good News Bible entitles Chapter 34, "The Rape of Dinah". There is *no* warrant in the text for calling what took place "rape". Dinah obviously *pretended* she was going to visit Canaanite girls, when she was secretly meeting her Hivite boyfriend. If she had been going to meet girlfriends, she is unlikely to have gone alone - a group would have gone to meet a group. If she was alone with the boy, she had planned to be. This lad loved her (v 3). Her father made sure she loved him; and drew up a marriage contract with his father, the Hivite chief. Dinah was living, presumably happily, with her husband, when the two brothers, responding to the judgmental murmurings of the others, went on their spree of massacring all the boys and men, who were lying sore in their tents, after the ritual circumcising. Jacob, their father, was *embarrassed* at the barbarity of it - it gave him a bad name amongst his neighbours (v 30), who, he was *afraid*, might attack him - but a verbal reprimand was all the punishment *they* received for their cowardly butchery of innocents. The Bible makes no apology for any of the vile atrocities of the Israelites on the Canaanites. Here it justifies them, saying, "the sons of Jacob answered Shechem and Hamor, his father, deceitfully", *as though this exonerates them from blame!* (34 v 13)

Massacre was what these two brothers saw as fit punishment for what they considered was a sexual crime against their sister *by one person*! Their murder of so many innocent people, they did *not* see as a crime. Their own sexual sins against the women and little girls that they take, along with everything else belonging to the tribe, are also *not* seen as sins or crimes. They have a blinkered attitude, that allows them to commit every dreadful act there is, but they are merciless to *others*, especially if the others are Canaanite. This attitude pervades the whole of the Old Testament! Sadly, it is not condemned in the New.

In fact, these brothers, from whom the tribes of Israel are named, are made honourable mention of in Christianity, as though their multiple murders do not matter. They should receive *dishonourable* mention because of their crimes against humanity! But Christianity has kept the Scriptures of the brothers' racist religion, written by their descendants, which, of course, praises them. Such lack of criticism cannot continue. Christianity has got to state that this Old Covenant, which engendered all kinds of murderous activity was *not* faith, but *self-interest*. None of the Canaanite nations mentioned in the Bible had vile racist views like the Israelites had. None!

The father, Jacob, had not intended to have so many wives, nor therefore, presumably, children. It had come about because the two wives, Leah and Rachel, had slaves, whom they were able to present to their husbands as concubines. The wives were greedy for children, and the slaves' children would be counted as their mistresses'. The jealousies and bickering between these four wives, with twelve sons and probably about twelve daughters to boot, can be easily imagined! Jacob, himself, gives the verdict on his life, when, seventeen years before he died, he met the Pharaoh of Egypt. "How old are you?" asked the Pharaoh. "I am only one hundred and thirty," he replied. "I have had a short, unhappy life!" (47 v 9)

Christians usually think that it was the famous "coat of many colours" (the translation, later corrected by scholars to read, "coat with long sleeves") that was the final straw, that tipped the brothers' animosity to Joseph over the edge. They think he was given the coat because he was his father's favourite. The father was probably not so stupid as to do that. Indeed, we are told in 1 Chronicles 5 v 1, the more likely reason for his receiving the coat: the rights of the firstborn were removed from Reuben for sleeping with his stepmother, Bilhah. Joseph was the firstborn of the second wife, Rachel, and the rights and privileges of the firstborn were given to him. Dan and Gad the firstborn of the concubines, Bilhah and Zilpah, could have felt aggrieved that they had been passed over, rubbing their noses in the fact that their mothers were slaves, with no rights. No wonder Jacob's verdict on his life was "unhappy", with all that potential for jealousy and family squabbling!

Each generation passed on to the next, Abraham's dream of many descendants and a Land. Self-interest and self-delusion are equated with faith in the New Testament assessment of their Old Testament founders and leaders. This is natural for those belonging to that tradition, but for the Christian tradition to be perpetuating those events as God acting in history is preposterous. Those people deceived themselves. We should not be allowing them, in the 21st century, to continue to deceive *us*!

Up to the end of Genesis, it is plain to see that the faith of the patriarchs is of blood sacrifices, in return for the desired favours of many descendants and a Land. These things were already happening for them - *the Canaanites allowed peaceful coexistence.* That could have continued - provided that numbers were kept down to what a small, partly desert country could support. Such *common sense* was not in the Israelites' heads. *Vast numbers*, completely unsustainable on such territory, were their wild imaginings. The numbers (perhaps two million people, plus animals to feed) that returned from Egypt, several hundred years after their *first* arrival - all because the brothers had sold Joseph as a slave - were such that they came like a pack of ravening wolves, and ate up the indigenous people.

But the Church teaches that those wolves were *God's people*, and that was *his plan*! It beggars belief!

CHAPTER 13

THE JEALOUS GOD

"I am a jealous God", says God to Moses, in Exodus 20 v 5, and the Church has happily gone along with this pathetic depiction of the Creator. "If the Bible says he is jealous, then he *must* be jealous, and it must be *right* for him to be jealous", is the circular logic operating here. What he is particularly jealous of is idols! Idol-worshippers, it came to be understood, were the lowest form of humanity, and even though the Israelites, from Rebecca to David, *also* had household gods, or idols, their own idol-worship was not classed as such! The Canaanites could be murdered with impugnity because they worshipped idols! The Church has traditionally agreed that this was valid religion, on the part of the Israelites! What kind of God it was (and *is*), who required "his" people to become sub-human in morality and in sensitivity, so that they could perpetuate the vilest crimes, is seldom asked in the Church - at least, not by Church leaders, only by the ordinary members..

The next all-important question, which our theologians, again, fail to ask is, "Is idol-worship worse than murder?" By failing to ask, let alone answer, that question, the Church assents to *murder*, to the extent of *genocide*. By failing to ask the question, it is saying that idol-worship *is* worse than murder - as long as you claim *God* told you to commit the atrocities! This is the *craziest* of theologies! There is an absolute *void* where there should be common sense, not to say *morality*.

The God which inspired such wickedness is worshipped in Christianity, whilst the idols which inspired kindness are vilified. The *opposite* should be the case: if God inspires immorality, would it not be better to worship the idols which do not? Judge by what the followers of each type of religion do in the Bible - the Canaanites welcome strangers, are friendly, give food, protect foreigners who come calling; the Israelites arrive and kill as many Canaanites as they can, in order to annihilate them, and steal everything - their Land, their food and their wealth. Which are better? The Canaanites! Christianity does not say so - it says the Israelites.

Instead of *rubbishing* this caricature of God that we have in the Old Testament, Christianity embraces it. Not only is this God *jealous*, he inspires *massacre*. Well, has *he* not already massacred in the Flood, and in the Plague of the Egyptian Firstborn? That, too, is accepted as all right in Christianity. It is time for the Church to admit there is something *far wrong* with its theology. It is *not acceptable* that the Church continues to teach the God of drowning, jealousy and war.

CHAPTER 14

VILLAINOUS HEROES: THE BOOK OF JUDGES

BARAK: JUDGES 4 & 5

This is another Israelite hero, totally inappropriate for Christianity. He is goaded by the prophetess, Deborah, into attacking more Canaanites for more land. Barak seems to be a bit reluctant to go on the attack, but, in the usual fashion, she assures him that God will be fighting with him, and that he will have the victory. To refuse her request would be like refusing God! Still, he is reluctant, unless she come too. (Now that was a good idea! What a pity *all* inciters to fight, do not have to go along to the battles, especially to the front line. Many people could have wished that, in many wars since!) As if to punish Barak for suggesting this, Deborah predicts that, although he will be victorious, he will not get the glory, for a woman will kill Sisera, the Canaanite army leader.

What Christian scholars call a "glorified account" of what happened is written in Judges 4 and 5. It is a sickening story of betrayal, by a Canaanite queen, of her own people. There is no glory, except to the Israelites, who would have the territory at all costs, and when the cost was thousands of Canaanite lives, that was an even better victory to them - for then they had the Land empty of people, but full of their wealth.

All this butchery purports to have been planned by God! How else could Deborah have foretold it? Easily! The story was embroidered in the retelling, with the prophecy inserted. It was written with hindsight, as well as bias.

GIDEON: JUDGES 6 - 8

Gideon's encounter with an *angel* is what inspires him to *fight*, and very idealistic he seems, at the beginning of his story. He talks to *God*, getting all his directions for slaughtering the Midianites, in whose Land he is living. Notice in passing that he is not starving in their Land, nor has he been killed by the indigenous people. He is living well in their Land, able to kill bulls for sacrifices and bake kilos of flour into bread, not for eating, but just to have burned up on a stone, allowing God to prove his power. Besides that, Gideon had wealth enough to be able to father and feed seventy-odd sons (and, presumably, daughters) - all *on Midianite territory*.

With so many offspring, more territory must *soon* become necessary. If *you* have that many children, you have to stop others from having *any*; it is a matter of economics and of arithmetic. And this God of economics and arithmetic has a policy of allowing others *no* progeny, especially if they are *Canaanites*, and God's man and God succeed in clearing the Land for the Israelites to populate, as usual. Gideon is offered the hereditary leadership of Israel, but refuses it, still giving God the honour. Instead, he asks for gold, and melts twenty kilograms of it into an idol, which encouraged idol-worship. Was that not supposed to make God jealous?

However, for all his consulting of God, he leaves a legacy of disaster, which hits not only the Canaanites. His fathering of so many children reaps a reward of family treachery, when Abimelech - whose mother was not one of the many wives, but a concubine (sex slave) living in another town - killed his seventy half-brothers, with only the youngest escaping. Civil war ensued amongst the Israelites.

Yet *this* is the hero whom a group of Christian businessmen, dedicated to furthering the cause of Bible knowledge, chose to name their organisation after. They obviously have a radically different understanding of the Bible and its characters from mine.

JEPHTHAH : JUDGES 10 - 12

Jephthah had been kicked out of his family, for being the son of a prostitute. The greedy, legitimate progeny were determined he would not inherit any of Gilead, his father's, property. Poor Jephthah had to fend for himself. As luck would have it, he was befriended by other outcasts, who evidently lived by banditry. Jephthah gained such a reputation as a thug, that, eventually, his family decided he was *just* what they needed to help them fight the Canaanites, who were trying to win back some of their territory.

But, in the Bible, fights about land are always called "the Lord's battles", and outcast or not, thug or not, Jephthah is sworn in as God's man, fighting for the *Lord*. Canaanites have no rights to anything, in the Bible, no right to their own Land, or houses, nor to bring up their families - no rights, except to be killed, if male, and misused, if female! Suddenly, Jephthah is a *religious* man, fighting the 'battles of the Lord'. And the Christian Church believes that!

There is a terrible sting in the tail, which makes this story stand out from the usual gloatings of the victors over the vanquished, the ruthless over the mild-mannered, the warlike over the peaceful... Jephthah had done a deal with God, as those going into battle generally did, in the Bible, and, perhaps still do, in modern times. He had made a promise to sacrifice the first person who walked out of his house when he got home. (The God of Israel obviously had an appetite for *human* sacrifices, as well as *animal* ones!)

No doubt Jephthah hoped it would be a slave, who would come out first to greet him, or an expendable wife, or concubine - but no - it was his sweet young daughter, dancing, and playing the tambourine! Making the story even more poignant, we are told she was his only child. This innocent was sacrificed to the *distortion* of God, that the Old Testament presents. Yet, the Church teaches that *this* God, of *land* and of *blood*, is righteous, moral, and "the Father of our Lord, Jesus Christ". Not good enough! There are different gods, named in the Bible, and the one named the 'God of Israel' is a God of blood and battles, an immoral God, the antithesis of the God of love for all mankind, and peace on Earth, represented by Jesus Christ.

SAMSON : JUDGES 14 - 16

The birth of this *hooligan* was, like so many others in the Bible, foretold by an *angel*, this one in the form of a man, who was willing to converse with the unhappy couple, whose future son would bring untold misery to thousands of Philistines, as well as quite a lot of trouble and heartache to his parents. No wonder - he was dedicated to a God of *kill and take*! How could anyone dedicated to *that* God turn out well? His mother was put on a special diet during her pregnancy, and the child was also specially fed and cared for - and spoilt rotten!

Among his hobbies - which seem to have consisted of killing and terrorising lions, foxes and the Philistines, in whose Land his family was living unmolested - was womanising. But, although he was the dedicated enemy of the Philistines, he lusted after their women, visiting prostitutes, and insisting, against his parents' wishes, on marrying two of the despised, uncircumcised nation. During negotiations for the first wedding, and for no good reason, he killed a young lion. This then became the subject of a riddle he put to some of the wedding guests. He hoped to win easily lots of clothes. However, his smart idea brought the marriage to a speedy end, for his poor wife became the innocent victim of his trick. The guests soon realised that it was daylight robbery on his part, implicated her, and threatened to kill her family if she did not find out the answer.

46

The wife got the answer to the riddle out of him, but Samson had no thoughts of *buying* outfits for the winners. He killed and stripped thirty innocent Philistines instead. What he did to his wife is not stated, but it was enough to let her father think he *hated* her, whereupon he married her to someone else - the man who had been best man at the wedding, Samson's friend.

But she and her family were doomed! To have dealings with such a man as Samson, this 'man of God', almost made that a certainty. This one-man-band of terror rampaged through Philistia, wreaking havoc wherever he went. His rage at hearing his wife had been given away to another, meant another spree of sickening violence, with the destruction of crops, animals and people, none of whom had anything to do with his failed marriage. He had caused the trouble there all by himself! A tit-for-tat episode ensued, in which the Philistines killed the bride and her family, for her connection with Samson, who used this as the excuse for yet more violence, killing another thousand men.

Yet, he insisted on marrying another Philistine, Delila. Like the previous wife, Delila also became the victim of the politics that lay behind Samson's actions. His ulterior motive was always to destroy as many Philistines as he could. His final accolade is that he killed even more Philistines in his *death*, than he had done in his *life* - people whose only crime was to live in the Land where they were born, another Land that the incomers wanted!

The Philistines were *civilised* in ways that the Israelites, for all their disparagement of them, could never hope to emulate. Samson had brothers, who were allowed to come and take the vicious terrorist's body home for a hero's burial. This was never allowed to any of the Israelites' victims. They made public exhibition of the kings they killed, and annihilated as many of each tribe as they could, removing the women, who were not allowed to bury or mourn their men or little boys. The Bible tells us so!

This hero of Church sermons and Sunday School lessons, this Samson, should be an *embarrassment* and *shunned*, but Christianity is so blind it will not see! Our ministers are good at selecting the passages they can cope with, ignoring those they cannot. Evidently "God's Chosen People" were not embarrassed, either, by his savagery against all forms of life - crops, animals, and human beings. How could they be? They were a disaster of the first magnitude that arrived in Canaan, just as Samson was a disaster that arrived in Philistia! But no atrocity embarrasses the writers of the Bible, for they incorporate the vilest deeds into their record of heroic (to them) tales, saying God decreed it. And the Church calls it "Holy Scripture"!

For children to be taught, as I was in Sunday School, to *rejoice* when thousands of Philistines were massacred, is to teach *immorality*. It is *child abuse*, to require children to do the mental gymnastics, indeed psychological contortions, they have to do, in order to see Samson and his ilk as godly men. It is also blasphemy to say that God, whom Christianity inconsistently says is *love*, inspired these massacres.

MICAH AND THE DANITES : JUDGES 17 & 18

This story clearly illustrates, not only the rapacious nature of people who thought they were so godly, they despised the religions of others, but also shows the quality of that religion.

Micah is *so* horrible, he steals a considerable amount of silver from his mother. However, when she, cleverly, puts a curse on the stolen silver, he gets worried and confesses. Thereupon, she tries to revoke the curse, by pronouncing a blessing on her son, and declaring the silver dedicated to the Lord. The way this was done was to have a silversmith work the silver into an idol and an image for the household shrine. This seems to be the same, in the religion, as worshipping The Lord. Micah now took to his religion in quite a big way, making an ephod, the vestment of a priest. He even installed his son as priest, until a real one, a lad belonging to the tribe of Levi, came alone, looking for a position. Micah appointed him the family priest, with a salary. He would wear the ephod and perform the rituals required by the Laws of Moses. We find out, at the end of the story, that this priest is even the grandson of Moses, Jonathan. All were happy, unless, perhaps, the ousted son - we are not told how he felt at losing his job.

What we are told next, is about the other aspect of Israelite religion, the seizing of land. Spies from the tribe of Dan come by, and are very interested in Micah's religious set-up, especially the silver. They take the opportunity to consult the priest about the outcome of their planned raid. He tells them they will be successful, and indeed, they are. They continue on their way, and come to a small town in very fertile country, with only a few peaceful and unsuspecting inhabitants. They return home with the news of an easy take, and bring six hundred armed men to attack the peaceful native population.

On the way, they stop off at Micah's house, and, since the five spies now have an army with them, they commandeer all the precious accoutrements of the shrine, including the priest, who is happy at the new job offer he receives from them, of being priest to a whole tribe, not just to a family. Micah protests, but they threaten to kill him and his family. Well, they would, wouldn't they, for they are *the Army of the Lord*? Thus he is left, with the curse on the silver, and the blessing on his life, having come to pass.

The story has a happy ending for the Danites. They get very good land for the easy massacre of just one town of peaceful people, Laish, which they rename Dan. *This* is the dream of Abraham and the religion of Moses in operation - threats and curses, stolen silver and gold, elaborate rituals performed by Levites, massacres of the rightful inhabitants of the Land, and resettlement of it by Israelites. This kind of religion should be a million miles away from Christianity, yet *this* religion is still *part* of Christian teaching!

The heroes of Judaism should *not* be seen as heroes in Christianity, nor should they be reckoned as godly men at all. "Deluded by indoctrination", is the best that Christianity should be saying about them! The true heroes of the Bible are the Canaanites; vilified and discounted as unimportant, even irrelevant, for so long, it is now high time for the Church to tell the *moral* truth, and take *their* side, belatedly, as *victims of an unjust religion*.

This is Liberation Theology.

CHAPTER 15

GOLIATH OF GATH: 1 SAMUEL 17 - 22

When poor little unarmed David faces up to the armoured and armed Goliath, the reader is automatically on the side of the little man against the giant. "Right against might", we think - and we think justice is served when the giant falls on the impact of David's slung stone. God is on the side of the oppressed against the oppressor, and that is how it should be, we think. It sounds very plausible - until we work out properly what is going on, and see what the bigger picture is.

Then we discover that this story belies the truth. David, in fact, represents an armed, ruthless aggressor, who came to wage war, whilst Goliath represents people who were being done to death for their Land, and did *not* seek war. They were, in fact, willing to *share* their Land with incomers. *Sharing* did not satisfy the invaders. Understanding *this* turns the usual view of the David and Goliath story on its head.

There were three tribes of tall people in Canaan, the Anakim (or Anakites), the Emim, and the Zamzummin. These were all also called by the name "Rephaim". The Zamzummin, we are told in Deuteronomy 2 v 21, were destroyed by the Ammonites, who took their territory. King Og's tribe of Anakites, on the East of the Jordan, was annihilated in the first wave of Israelite attacks, under Moses. We are told they captured sixty fortified cities, as well as countless villages, putting every man, woman and child to death, and plundering their possessions (Deut. 3 v 6). This massacre is recounted, as are all the other massacres of the Canaanites, with chilling matter-of-factness, and a complete lack of pity or remorse, which becomes even more appalling, when one remembers that the Christian Church has taught all of these massacres, for two thousand years, as good, right, directed by God, and therefore, "holy"!

Goliath and the other giants, alive at the time of David, must have been the remnant, left after the Joshua attacks on the Anakites of the Hebron area. We are told that they were wiped out in the territory which the Israelites controlled, but that there were a few living in the Philistine cities of Ashdod, Gath and Gaza (Joshua 11 v 22).

The Israelites believed them to have been descended from the mythical Nephilim - the "sons of God", who descended from the Heavens, and fathered children by women, whose beauty they could not resist (Genesis 6 v 1 - 4)! Not that this

50

heavenly parentage weighed anything with the Israelites when it came to the matter of *land*! There was only *one* policy for those inhabiting land they wanted, and that was "Exterminate, exterminate"! A few, a very few, seem to have been able to flee to Philistia, which, in the time of David, became the Land the Israelites would fight for, again, with ruthless determination.

Who has ever heard a sermon on the Nephilim? Not many people, I dare say! The consorting of the "heavenly beings", with the beautiful women was before the Flood which was supposed to have drowned everyone except Noah's family. We might then ask, "So the giants also survived the Flood?" But we should not attempt to apply logic to ancient myths. The Bible itself gets round the problem of logic neatly, by saying, "There were giants in the land in those days, *and also after that*" (Gen. 6 v 4)!

After those few verses about the "sons of God" making their appearance in history, the folklore changes to visitations from "angels", who usually look like ordinary men, but, in the visionary writings, often appear dressed in (white) linen, sometimes having wings (Isaiah 6 v 2). Two of them are even given the rank of Archangel (higher than just "angel",and *names*, Michael and Gabriel (Daniel 8 v 17; 10 v 13). And Michael has a *job* - Israel's Guardian Angel! This angelology continues in the New Testament, especially in the book of Revelation.

The Philistines knew they had a formidable enemy, when the Israelites arrived on their borders. These had relentlessly been moving westwards, killing everyone in their wide path for more than two hundred years, and now the Philitines' territory was the one in the Israelites' sights. The Philistines did not ask for this war - *none* of the Canaanite nations had looked for a fight. There are many examples to show they always welcomed the Israelites amongst them. Samson had moved around their lands and cities freely. David, also, lived with them, when it suited him, and, *even though* they knew he was their enemy, they picked no fight with him. More than that, he knew *he was safer with the Philistines than with the Israelites* - that is how lovely, gracious, and hospitable the Philistines were. The Canaanites and Philistines are the beautiful people of the Bible. They are the *civilised* ones, kind and welcoming. They are the vilified ones, but *they* are the godly ones!

When the Philistine and Israelite armies lined up for battle on the day David, youngest son of Jesse, arrived from home with food for his brothers, he heard Goliath, one of the few remaining descendants of the "sons of God" (according to Hebrew Scripture), issue a challenge for single combat. Doubtless, he thought he would win, but, at the same time, his offer was a generous one, for it offered the assurance of *life* to the ordinary soldiers on both sides, apart from the one he might kill. Both armies then could disband, and go home to their anxious families.

This humane offer had no hope of being understood by the Israelites. It was not an accommodation with the enemy that they wanted, with mutually agreed land for each nation so that they could live side by side. *That was never in the Israelites' thoughts. That* was only in the *Philistines'* thoughts. The 'Chosen People of God' were never so amenable, or open to reason.

If Goliath had won the fight with David, the Philistines would have allowed the Israelite army to go home. All the information we have of their character indicates this. Not so, the Israelites! When David is victorious, they cash in on his victory, in the barbaric way we are used, too used, to reading about! They pursue the retreating Philistines, hacking them to death as they flee homeward.

The Philistines had allowed Samson's family to collect his body from their capital city, and take it home. Goliath's family was not accorded this consolation. Reciprocity was never practised. The Israelites always made barbaric exhibition of leaders they killed. Goliath's head was taken for public gloating over in Jerusalem.

Much is made in Christian teaching, of Goliath's defiance of Israel's God, and 'the Lord's' army (1 Samuel 17 v 45) - as though he had not *every right* to speak against this God and people, who were intent on continuing their policy of killing all his folk. The Christian Church, too, should defy and decry such a God and such an army! They are *not* compatible with the rest of its teaching. It should *salute Goliath*, as a victim of a distortion of God, and of godless hate!

CHAPTER 16

DAVID: 1 SAMUEL 16 - 2 SAMUEL 24

"That great man, after God's own heart", says Bible commentator, Matthew Henry, of David. How would he know that? Well - he would judge by what he has learned of God in the book he is commenting on, and he has *accepted* the double-tongued, harsh, murdering monster, depicted there, as God - and sees the likeness in David. Well spotted, Mr Henry! He does *not* discern that this is a *travesty* of God, as hundreds of thousands of people in Scotland have discerned, and have stopped attending church because they cannot stomach the *caricature*!

David shoots to fame in Israel when he kills Goliath. This is one of the most popular Bible stories for telling to children. It is encouragement to the weak to face up to the strong, the humble to the proud, the faithful to the faithless, etc. David is forever "God's man", however two-faced, however cruel, however murderous, however spiteful, however adulterous - all is forgiven David, because he killed Goliath, and because he wrote some Psalms, and said some prayers when he was feeling afraid, or guilty, or wanting God's protection from King Saul, or help to kill *yet more* Canaanites and Philistines... Some God, this God of David!

The story of the slaying of Goliath *ought* to be told as a lucky strike for David, in a war of attrition, when a ruthless invader came against an innocent nation, determined to take its Land. Instead, it is told by the Church as God guiding the stone from David's sling, right to Goliath's vulnerable spot, at his temple. All the slaughter and gloating that takes place in the story is approved by God! David found his role in life when he joined in "The Lord's War" against the Philistines. In any other context, a murderous invader would be condemned. In the context of this religion, however, murderous invaders claim God on their side, wage what they call "Holy War", where crimes against humanity are at their most barbaric, and, with infamy heaped upon injury, *stupid people believe them*! Well - it is time that Christians no longer believed them.

The Israelites saw their attacks on the Philistines as "Holy War". They even had a book called "The Book of the Wars of the Lord", lost long ago, mentioned in Numbers 21 v 14! From Abraham on, *their* wishes and *their* doings were equated with *God's* wishes and *God's* doings. No distinction is made between the two: *their* mind is always claimed to be *God's* mind!

But let us be clear - *there is no such thing as holy war.* War is always *unholy!* Do not confuse "Holy War" with "Just War". The Philistines were fighting a Just War, because they were defending themselves against an aggressor. They had no choice. This war was *thrust* upon them. They were acting only to defend their lives, their families and their Land. A "Just War" can only be fought in self-defence: it cannot be invasion and attack. There *may* be other definitions, fulfilling certain conditions, as first suggested by St Thomas Aquinas in the 13th century. These conditions, now increased from his suggested three to five, are generally agreed as;

the war must

1, be called and controlled by the State, or ruler;

2, have a just cause;

3, have a goal of promoting good, or avoiding evil - peace and justice being restored afterwards

4, be a last resort, after all other solutions have been tried; and

5, keep the level of violence as low as possible; this being called "proportionality".

The trouble with such a set of conditions is that they are open to interpretation, therefore, controversy, and also, abuse. A "just cause" could be *imagined*, or even engineered, as an *excuse* for attack. However, the very fact of attack, gives the other side *just cause* to fight. People have a right to defend themselves!

In this unspeakably cruel war, totally unsought by the Philistines, they are made absolute fools of by David, who *uses* their hospitality, their generosity, their guilelessness and their trust of him - as we shall see - and, even though the history is written by their sworn enemy, *yet* it has not been able to hide the beautiful character of the Philistines, undeserving of the execration unleashed upon them. Just as students of Shakespeare lament and puzzle over Iago's hatred of Othello and Desdemona, and his vile plan to "turn her virtue into pitch, and out of her own goodness make the net that shall enmesh them all", so Bible students should lament David's evil machinations against kind people, and deplore his determination to bring them down - so, also, the vile treatment of the *hospitable* Canaanites at the hands of the Israelite nation. This would be Liberation Theology.

The trouble begins, as we might guess, with *deceit* in the religion. David is anointed King of Israel, secretly, by the prophet Samuel, who has gone off Saul, whom he has previously anointed King. (Thus the prophet has anointed two kings - a recipe for trouble!) He had chosen Saul for his height, and this time, he was determined not to make the same mistake, "for man looketh on the outward appearance, but the Lord looketh on the heart", (1 Sam. 16 v 7). He promptly chose by outward appearance again, kidding himself that he was not, because David was not tall - yet he was, "of a beautiful countenance"(v 12).

Could anything give a person more self-confidence than to know he was "God's anointed"? Hardly! It is not surprising, then, that "the spirit of the Lord came upon David from that day on", (v 13) - this equates to a spirit of *eagerness to kill* every Philistine and Canaanite he could! Unfortunately for Saul, the Lord's spirit left him - just when he needed it *most* (fickle Lord!), with a rival in his camp, and a mental affliction of terrible fits of depression. Worse than that, if the Lord gave him an evil spirit (v 15), it indicates that the writer of the embroidered history that we have in this book, *knows* this God *administers evil!*

David, also, knows that at least some of his killings are crimes. He admits as much in Ch 25 v 33, although he does not see extortion - lack of compliance with which, was going to be the excuse for his near murder of Nabal and his family - as at all reprehensible. So much for the Spirit of the Lord in him! But any guilt he feels is limited only to the murder of fellow *Israelites*. He felt no guilt about the death of Uriah the Hittite (albeit in David's army) until the Prophet Nathan forced him to admit he had done wrong. Indeed, to kill *Canaanites* and Philistines, he sees as his religious duty, viz. the bride price he paid Saul for Michal, of two hundred Philistine foreskins (18 v 25)! No quibble - yet he could have quibbled, for he had been promised, along with tax exemption for his family, the King's eldest daughter in marriage, as a reward for killing Goliath. What did it matter if it was a different daughter, one who loved him? All the better! But he *chose* to kill two hundred Philistines, and *not* quibble - killing Philistines was a favourite pastime, besides a religious duty!

Much is made, in Christian teaching, of David's great character, in refusing to harm Saul, when he had chances to kill him (Ch 24 & 26), and, of course, of his great *faith*, evidenced in the Psalms, most of which he is credited with writing. In many ways, David does show admirable qualities in respect of Saul, although, his insistence not to kill 'the Lord's anointed' could, also, be vested interest. He, too, is anointed, and he knows his day will come. If *he* was prepared to kill the Lord's anointed, he could hardly complain if, one day, someone killed him. In any case, Saul is still his father-in-law, and the father of his best friend, Jonathan. The fact is, however, David's *religion* turned a perfectly nice lad, into a *warrior*, full of *hate* and *cruelty* towards innocent people, and he could not see that killing as many of them as possible, was not virtuous. He was a sincere man, but sincerely *wrong!*

As for his faith in God - it is faith in a *cruel monster* who protects him doing his dirty work! It would be more to David's credit if he had seen that! Many mass-murderers, up to the present day, have been, and are, very religious. In the case of this religion, it is *terrorism in disguise*, and *racist* terrorism at that! David's real religion was killing Philistines, and that was terrorism. *That* was the religion he inherited.

Although he has killed "tens of thousands" of them, yet they show him the most amazing hospitality, which he abuses, when he goes to live in Philistia, with his wives and army of six hundred men! What a calamity for a nation to have stupid leaders! Gath had a very gullible king, who was always completely taken in by David's lies. King Achish took the murderer into his own kingdom, even making David his personal bodyguard! The biggest *killer* of Philistines becomes *bodyguard* of a Philistine King - that is one *fool* of a king! He gives David whatever he asks for, and he asks for a town. He was given Ziglag, and kept it (27 v 6).

Banditry is also taken several stages further into evil with David. During his sixteen-month stay in Philistia, he substantially weakened his hosts, by systematically wiping out their neighbours and allies. As usual, he left *no one alive* to tell what he was up to, and pretended to King Achish that he was raiding in Southern Judah, i.e. his own nation. Achish believed him (v 12)! Luckily for the Philistines, their other kings had more sense. When it came to another battle with Israel, under Saul, David was keen to fight alongside Achish. However, the kings of the other four Philistine cities, suspecting the treachery that would surely have ensued, refused to have David with them. Thus, they lived to fight another day, in yet another battle forced upon them.

It is "take your pick" as to which account of the death of Saul you believe, for there are two contradictory reports, in 1 Samuel Ch 31, and 2 Samuel Ch 1 - an amalgamation of two different records. The saddest part of both of the stories is the unnecessary death of a young man. The first account says that he witnessed Saul's death, and killed himself. The second says that he brought the news of it to David, who had the messenger killed for bringing the bad news! This fits the character of David, especially as the messenger was Amalekite. David self-righteously refers to this slaying, when he has Ishbosheth's two murderers summarily executed (2 Sam 4). The difference is that the two had *murdered* the man, the Amalekite had *not*; he had only obeyed Saul's request to put him out of his misery, and not let him be captured, fatally wounded, by the Philistines. David did not make a distinction.

In a single chapter, 2 Samuel Ch 8, always with *the Lord* inspiring, directing, and giving victory, David kills more than sixty thousand Syrians and Edomites, as well as unnumbered Philistines and Moabites! He cripples horses he captures, but cannot use. Yet, in v 15, we are told of his fair dealings with the people. This can only refer to *men* belonging to the twelve tribes of Israel. There was *no* justice for women, or for the indigenous tribes. This God cannot be made palatable to people who believe God has to be for *all* and not just *some* - especially when the "some", supposedly doing God's will, are bloodthirsty in the extreme, and unwholesomely interested in gold, silver, bronze, precious jewels, loot of all kinds, and, above everything else, *land*!

For a man "after God's heart", David's treatment of women is disgraceful. To his credit, he refused the offer of his prize, mentioned earlier, of Saul's eldest daughter, and then married, for love, one of his younger daughters, Michal (18 v 20). Hers was an impossible position, with her father insanely jealousy of her husband, forcing him to flee his home, and go into hiding (19 v 17). Married or not, her father gave her to a man who loved her better than David, who had, meanwhile, taken two more wives (25 v 44). Out of spite David had Michal dragged away from her distraught husband (2 Sam 3 v 16), to bury her, neglected to the end of her days, in his ever-increasing harem (5 v 13). His love for her had soon turned to hate!

David's terrible family split with his son, Absalom, was *supposed* to be because of the curse put upon him by Nathan the prophet, for his sin in arranging for Uriah's death (2 Sam 12 v 11) to cover up his adultery. In fact, it was the direct result of his disgraceful failure to punish his son, Amnon for raping his half-sister, Tamar, Absalom's beautiful full sister (Ch 13). This inaction on the father's part must have increased the grief and rage that Absalom and his sister had to deal with. The result was not only a family rift, but civil war with the tribe of Judah, when Absalom got the other tribes to follow him, and proclaimed himself King. Before the matter was concluded twenty-two thousand men were dead, and Absalom, himself, caught by his long, thick hair in a tree, was set upon like hounds on a wounded fox, by his cousin Joab, who was David's Army Commander, and ten of his soldiers.

Not *every* Canaanite male possible was put to death in David's reign, as they had been in the time of Moses and Joshua (apart from the Gibeonites). He spared some Moabites, killing only two out of three prisoners, and making the remnant pay taxes to him (2 Sam 8 v 2). Well might he have spared some Moabites! The King of Moab had been a refuge to him, in his days of danger from Saul. He had left his parents with the King of Moab for safety! And *this* was how he repaid the hospitable Moabites - by attacking them, and letting *some* live, to pay him tribute! His great grandmother, Ruth, was Moabite! Shame, shame, shame! Nationality or race should not have mattered at all, anyway. We are all *people*. But to the Israelites, nationality was *everything*! God was *theirs*, exclusively, and did not love anyone else - because *they* did not!

No wonder King Hannun of Ammon did not trust David's gesture of sympathy and friendship, when his father died (Ch 10)! He had every justification *not* to! But David was aggrieved at the insult of his messengers having half their beards shaved off, and their clothes cut off at the hips, and sent home. Uh-oh - this loss of face *had* to mean another battle! It seems that lining up, and facing each other up, with reinforcements ready, on both sides, was enough to satisfy the hurt pride. This time there were no reported deaths - for a change!

For all David's protestations of not harming Saul, the Lord's anointed, he disposes of his *grandchildren* with remarkable calmness - or rather, *God* arranges for the deaths of Saul's descendants (21 v 1). (It is a very useful ploy to blame God...) The excuse (not reason) given, is that Saul killed the Gibeonites, descendants of those who had tricked Joshua into letting them live, and to whom the Israelites had made a sacred promise (Josh 9 v 20). Saul was a *murderer*, because he had killed some of them, so Saul's *innocent* grandchildren have to die, says God (= David). And their poor mothers, like the concubine, Rizpah, are driven out of their minds in this male-dominated, *unholy* society that calls itself "holy" and "righteous". Are not *all the Israelites* who plunged knives into men, women and children, *also murderers*? Have they not *all* broken their own commandment, which says, "Thou shalt not kill"? What crazy, convenient logic operates in this horrible, "holy" history? Oh, of course - killing *non*-Israelites does not count as murder, or "killing" - *that* logic!

Nathan, the prophet, is admired in Christian sermons, for his famous parable of the poor man's lamb, taken by the rich man - the story he told David, to illustrate his sin in the Bathsheba episode. Who has not been stirred by his courageous accusation, "You are the man" (12 v 7)? But Nathan's false platitudes in 2 Sam 7 have gone entirely unnoticed by the Church, which takes the words at face value, without applying any discernment or moral judgment. The Good News Bible translates part of it thus, "I (God) have chosen a place for my people Israel and have settled them there, where they will live without being oppressed any more. Ever since they entered this Land, they have been attacked by violent people."

The very *opposite* is the truth. *Abraham* chose the place - a *man*, not God. God did not settle them there - *they* did, by brutality, barbarity and butchery! They were *not* attacked by violent people. *They* were the violent people, and they attacked *peaceful* people. *That* is how the Church should teach the Bible. *The truth is reversed here*, and the Church has not noticed. It is preoccupied, ludicrously, by seeing David as a forerunner of Christ, with Christ fulfilling the prediction in v 16, "Your dynasty will last for ever". No - the whole of Nathan's speech here is *falsehood*!

David's deathbed scene, as told in the first chapters of 1 Kings, is as sickening as his violent life. It is not his fault that his aides search for the most beautiful virgin to come and warm him in bed, even though he has many neglected wives and concubines. Nor had the poor girl, of course, any right to refuse her unsavoury task of attempting to enliven a dying man.

The flesh was weak by then, but his mind was lively enough, even on his deathbed, to order the deaths of *more* men - Israelites this time. Although David had, at one point, replaced Joab as his Army Commander, he proved not to be so easily got rid of, for he promptly slew his successor Amasa (2 Sam 20 v 9), saying, "How are you, my friend?" making as if to kiss him! It suited David quite well to have his bloodthirsty nephew in charge of the army, yet he gave an instruction to Solomon to kill him "for killing innocent men", army chiefs, Abner and Amasa. Ironically, it seems no one ever told him that Joab had run Absalom through with three spears, whom David stressed, was *not* to be harmed (18 v 14). Why *should* anyone have told him? It would probably have meant the *messenger's* death as well!

Deceitful to the last, and showing what a long memory he had, he instructed Solomon, also, to have Shimei put to death, a man who had insulted him as he fled from Jerusalem during the trouble with Absalom (Ch 16). Shimei later apologised profusely, fearing execution for what he had said, but David was in magnanimous mood the day he returned to Jerusalem, and generously said, "I solemnly swear before the Lord, you will not die" (19 v 23). He evidently thought that by getting *Solomon* to arrange his murder, he was not breaking his vow - but he was!

Famous in the Church for his wisdom, and his peaceful reign (because Joab and David, between them, had killed practically every male in the Lands round about - see 1 Kings 11 v 16), Solomon's first actions as King were to arrange for the above-mentioned executions. For good measure, he had his half-brother, Adonijah, killed also, for daring to ask to marry the beautiful Abishag, who had been in bed with David before he died. Presumably, Solomon wanted her for himself - one among his seven hundred wives, and three hundred concubines, according to verse 3. Many of these women were Canaanite, probably the youngest and prettiest of those captured in David's wars, virgins, who were not, as the married women were, done to death.

King Solomon was able to enjoy a reign of peace, simply because his predecessors had engaged in so much warfare, and had left very few men, of the indigenous people, alive. He was given the task of building the Temple in Jerusalem, forbidden to his father, ostensibly because of his wars - but more probably to let some cedars grow again in Lebanon, as David had used them all up on his palaces. However, Christians should not be in any doubt - this peace was built on the foundation of a *holocaust on Canaan*. Moreover, this "man of peace" began his reign in the fine style of his father, David, by killing many *to order*, and by killing his half-brother from *choice*.

Such are our Christian heroes in the Bible!

CHAPTER 17

THE OCCULT: NUMBERS 22 - 25; 1 SAMUEL 28

The Occult is banned in the Bible. Human sacrifice, divination, horoscopes, spells, charms, witchcraft, wizardry, mediums, spiritists, and consulting the dead are all specifically outlawed in Deuteronomy 18 v 9 - 13. However, magic powers are, reportedly, given by God to some of his servants, to give them standing with the people - the Church *not* calling them *magic*, of course, but *miracle*. Thus, Moses was given power to turn his stick into a snake, and back again; water into "blood", and back again (Exodus 4). Pharaoh's magicians are able to do similar tricks, but are demonstrated to be inferior to Moses, since they could not do the returning part. Elijah was able to bring life back to a dead boy, and fire to wet wood (1 Kings 17 & 18). Sometimes angels come and perform miracles, reminiscent of magic tricks, as with Gideon (Judges 6 v 21).

In the New Testament there are two "sorcerers"; Simon, in Acts 8, who becomes a Christian, but fails to live up to Peter's expectations of him, and is at the receiving end of some harsh words; and Elymas, in Acts 13, who is accused by Paul of being a "child of the Devil...an enemy of righteousness...perverting the ways of the Lord". This is the Church's position on the Occult.

The most popular use of the Occult, both in Bible and in modern times, is to have the future foretold. The Israelites were no different from their neighbours in this, and regularly took steps to try to see into the future. You might think that their religion would say, "Trust in God, and do *not* try to see the future", but, not so, and there were three ways of finding out things *hidden* - which is what "occult" means. Thus, the religion of the Old Testament, although banning the Occult, has the Occult built into it - only, the religion calls it "consulting the Lord"!

How is the Lord consulted? The three ways were; by dreams, by consulting a priest, who used the Urim and Thummim (which scholars think were something like dice, used in such a way as to get answers to questions), and by consulting a prophet, sometimes called "the seer" - one who sees. These do not seem so radically different from some of the banned practices. Certainly, they are the same in one aspect, which is, that they try to know what the future holds, rather than trust in God and do right, which is what the Church teaches we should do.

61

Why have a Moral Code, if not to live by? The Ten Commandments are *not* the basis of behaviour in the religion of the Old Testament. Idol-worship (although it, also, is banned) as in Judges 17 v 3, superstition, blood rituals, sometimes even human sacrifice, as we have seen - *these* are the mainstay of the religion. Consulting those who predict the future, the prophets and priests, is part of it. Some of the modern translations indicate an inconsistency in the Law, as to the punishment for indulging in occult practices. The Good News Bible (Leviticus 19 v 31) states that those who consult mediums are ritually unclean, which means they can go through prescribed rituals to become clean again - but Ch 20 v 27 says clearly, that the penalty, both for consulting, and for giving the consultation, is death.

However, the Law does not seem to have been always rigorously applied - no wonder, when most of the punishments were capital - and indulging in the Occult was evidently widespread, when King Saul decided to clean up his country. The death penalty was going to be enforced, and so witches, sorcerers, and the like, had to flee to another town, where their spiritist activities were not so widely known about.

THE WITCH OF ENDOR: 1 Samuel 28

"Inconsistent" is the word that most aptly describes King Saul - and, of course, the time comes when he wants to consult a medium. He seeks one out, hiding in the town of Endor. Disguised or not, Saul was instantly recognisable, because he was a head bigger than anyone else in the country. The woman is terrified, but he promises she will not be punished.

Church ministers tend to avoid preaching on this passage, but I did hear one, who believed that the Witch of Endor really did call up the ghost of the dead prophet, Samuel, and that he gave her a message for King Saul. This goes completely *against* what the Church teaches about the Occult, for it says that it is "of the devil", and cannot, either predict the future, or contact the dead. Indeed, it is in total contradiction to the Christian teaching of the dead *resting in God*, awaiting Judgment Day.

Where was the spirit called from? It was called up - from under the Earth, presumably from Sheol, the shady underworld of Hebrew belief, where the dead went for a time, until they finally faded out of existence.

The message for Saul from the figure the woman conjures up, in her trance, is bad. It was common knowledge that Samuel (and therefore *God*) had fallen

62

out with the Anointed One (the King). During the latter part of his lifetime, Samuel had not had a kind word to say about him, and so, bad news could be expected. But how do Christian professors deal with *this* bad news - *The King had not been bad enough*, and *that* was why God was so angry with him? The King had actually (perhaps) shown a little *kindness*, and this was *anathema* to Samuel and to God! 1 Sam 28 v 18-"You ... did not completely destroy the Amalekites and all that they had..." He and his sons would die the next day. (The Occult has a fascination with death.)

The Old Testament, too, has a fixation with death, from the threat by God in Genesis 2 v 17, his massacre of most living things in the Flood, his massacring of Moses' opponents, be they Egyptian or Israelite, his inspiring of the massacres in Canaan, and the many death penalties for offending this oversensitive God!

CURSES

Curses are a prevalent feature of the Occult, and curses feature greatly in the Bible. As early as Genesis 3 v 14, God curses the snake; in v 17, he curses the ground, before going on to call down pain, hard work, thorns, weeds, and general suffering on everyone and everything forever.

Noah, in his disgusting life of debauchery, curses his grandson Canaan, unfairly, because he is angry with Canaan's father, Ham. (Gen. 9). Nasty people often vent their nastiness on the innocent. This nastiness can be in the form of a vow to God, a pretence of religious zeal, as with Japheth, when he sacrificed his daughter (Judges 11).

Threats and curses abound in the Old Testament, but the New Testament does not escape them. Jesus did not only teach love, forgiveness and Heaven, but threatened Hell as the punishment for hypocrisy. Even a fig tree, reputedly, came under his curse for not bearing fruit - which seems a bit much.

THINGS HIDDEN

Millions of Christian ministers' sermons have had as their subject the *name,* or refusal of a name, of God at the Burning Bush encounter with Moses in Exodus 3. "How wise, how significant, to call himself *I am that I am* ", they say. What rot! The very idea of God having a name, besides "God", is ludicrous! The fact that Moses asks for one, demeans God, putting him on a par with idols, who had names. God is *God*, and cannot possibly have a name, apart from God! The very idea of gods and demons with names is occult. The names Satan,

Lucifer, and Beelzebub have found their way into the Bible from ancient, occult folklore.

The "Occult", by definition, exults in secrecy, with only a chosen few "in the know". Several parts of the Bible are apocalyptic literature, notably parts of the books of Daniel and Ezekiel, in the Old Testament, and Revelation, in the New Testament. Contrary to the name, *Revelation*, this is a book of dreams and visions, of things *not* revealed, but hidden. The very name of it tries to hide the nature of the book - reminiscent of the Occult!

THE STORY OF BALAAM: Numbers 22 - 24

The idea of a "Chosen Nation", close to God, with other nations odious to this God, is offensive, and not to be countenanced - but this is the idea at the heart of this story.

The brutality of the Israelites was famous whilst they were still on their desert jouneyings, having not yet crossed the Jordan River into the "Promised Land". They went around slaughtering people for land that was *not* even part of what *they said* they had been promised. Yet, they still claimed God was guiding and helping them in the slaughter, *outside of the alleged promise* - and the Church has consistently *failed to condemn*, or even *notice* this, so innured is the Church to all the barbarity. This is unforgivable - but so are many other sins of the Church, such as the Crusades and the Conquistadors.

News of Israelite atrocities had reached Moab, and the people there were terrified, when they realised theirs was the next place on the bulldozers' route. Superstition was rife, and the people were desperate, realising they could soon be past tense. The most famous *medium* was Balaam, in Syria. King Balak of Moab sent messengers, with money for his fee, requesting that he come to Moab, and pronounce a curse on the invader. Balaam consults God (2), who does not seem to know anything about the emissaries from Moab. Once Balaam explains the situation to him, he is first told not to go (v 12), then to go (v 20), then not to go (v 32), then to go (v 35)! "What a changeable God this is", we may say.

This indecisive God gets angry when Balaam is on the journey, although he has just given permission to him to go. He sends an angel to bar the donkey's path, and the animal stops. The poor donkey receives three severe beatings from its master, before it, in righteous indignation, speaks, and so does the angel! In the three-way conversation that ensues, the donkey protests, the angel threatens, and Balaam says he has *sinned* for not knowing the invisible angel was standing on the road! (NB - massacres are *not* sins in this book, but not knowing an invisible angel is standing on the road *is* sin! Its values are completely haywire.)

Much building of altars, and slaughtering of bulls and rams take place, during which the King pleads for curses, whilst Balaam refuses to curse. (We have to remember who wrote this story...) In his messages, he describes himself as a clairvoyant, "one who sees clearly" (in a trance) (Num. 24 v 4 & 16) - a practitioner of the Occult. The author also puts into his mouth predictions of conquests by the Israelites, with God's help and blessing, and of the annihilation of the other nations.

For all his refusal to curse Israel, predicting, instead the wiping out of the Moabite King and his nation, with the others, it found him no favour with the Israelites. He was a victim in the mass killings on King Sihon's territory. His obituary, in Joshua 13 v 22, disparages him as much as all the others in the grim, sanctimonious reports of the annihilation of the native people - "the soothsayer" is the curt mention given him.

The New Testament continues in the same vein; 2 Peter 2 attributes a long list of sins to people like Balaam, "who loved the wages of unrighteousness" (v17). The writer totally fails to see that the sins listed are all those practised by the Israelites themselves. Neither does the Church discern this. Jude 11 says the same thing, and Revelation 2 v 14 *outrageously* blames Balaam for the idol-worship and sexual sins of the Israelites! They blame their own sins on others all the time.

The incident referred to is reported in Num. 25, when twenty-four thousand Israelites died from an epidemic. The outbreak was linked, whether accurately or hearsay, to the men having sexual intercourse with Moabite women. The inference is that the immoral women of Peor enticed the poor, unsuspecting Israelites into bed - *by the thousand*! This can only be a preposterous misrepresentation of what really happened. Certainly, according to the Bible account, there was hardly a male left alive in Canaan, after the arrival of the rot! The very idea of God having a name, besides "God", is ludicrous! The fact that Moses asks for one, demeans God, putting him on a par with idols, who had names. God is *God*, and cannot possibly have a name, apart from God! The very idea of gods and demons with names is occult. The names Satan, Lucifer, and Beelzebub have found their way into the Bible from ancient, occult folklore.

The "Occult", by definition, exults in secrecy, with only a chosen few "in the know". Several parts of the Bible are apocalyptic literature, notably parts of the books of Daniel and Ezekiel, in the Old Testament, and Revelation, in the New Testament. Contrary to the name, *Revelation*, this is a book of dreams and visions, of things *not* revealed, but hidden. The very name of it tries to hide the nature of the book - reminiscent of the Occult!

THE STORY OF BALAAM: Numbers 22 - 24

The idea of a "Chosen Nation", close to God, with other nations odious to this God, is offensive, and not to be countenanced - but this is the idea at the heart of this story.

The brutality of the Israelites was famous whilst they were still on their desert jouneyings, having not yet crossed the Jordan River into the "Promised Land". They went around slaughtering people for land that was *not* even part of what *they said* they had been promised. Yet, they still claimed God was guiding and helping them in the slaughter, *outside of the alleged promise* - and the Church has consistently *failed to condemn*, or even *notice* this, so innured is the Church to all the barbarity. This is unforgivable - but so are many other sins of the Church, such as the Crusades and the Conquistadors.

News of Israelite atrocities had reached Moab, and the people there were terrified, when they realised theirs was the next place on the bulldozers' route. Superstition was rife, and the people were desperate, realising they could soon be past tense. The most famous *medium* was Balaam, in Syria. King Balak of Moab sent messengers, with money for his fee, requesting that he come to Moab, and pronounce a curse on the invader. Balaam consults God (2), who does not seem to know anything about the emissaries from Moab. Once Balaam explains the situation to him, he is first told not to go (v 12), then to go (v 20), then not to go (v 32), then to go (v 35)! "What a changeable God this is", we may say.

This indecisive God gets angry when Balaam is on the journey, although he Israelites, but perhaps still some in surrounding territories like Moab. Although accommodating, the Moabite population was not likely to put up with Israelite men coming by the thousand into their Land to consort with their women. Not at all! The Israelites' normal practice,after an attack on a tribe, was to round up the girls, virgins, after the males and the married females had been massacred. Doubtless rape took place here, as everywhere else. The traumatised and grieving girls obviously received no sympathy for their plight, and were even blamed for the Israelites' diseases! Could more grievous insult ever be added to most grievous injury? The pattern of how the men, boys, male babies, and married women were killed, and the young females dealt out to the Israelite males, is described in Numbers 31.

A perverted view of God, hatred of non-Israelites, and cursing, continue throughout the Old Testament and into the New. This needs to be admitted by the Church. If God does not inspire brotherly love, compassion, openness, justice, mercy, forgiveness and enhance life, we do not want him. Throw out the theology of hate, with its cursing and killing. Teach love and life, not hatred and death!

CHAPTER 18

WOMEN OF THE OLD TESTAMENT

EVE, Genesis 2 - 4

Why is Adam, and not Eve, held responsible for eating the fruit, in the Garden of Eden story, thus causing "The Fall of *Man*"? It can only be that, in the eyes of the formulators of doctrine in the Church, Eve belongs to that sub-species of human being, woman. Although Eve gets *blame*, Adam is held *responsible*. It would be demeaning to have a woman responsible, according to the thinking of the all-male clergy in all traditions of the Church of yesteryear, and even of this year, in some Christian denominations.

Milton, in his poem PARADISE LOST, makes the disobedient two say plenty, but it is poetic licence. All we know of Eve from the Genesis story, is that she yielded to temptation, like her man, and was punished. If we really believed the doctrine of *The Fall*, we would have real cause to feel aggrieved at her, for, according to that doctrine, not only every person who has lived since, but the whole of Nature, is under condemnation. We suffer pain, we have to work hard, weeds, thorns, death and the horrible threat of eternal damnation - all our woes come from *her*. However, it is a *story*, as opposed to *history*, and *God* comes out of it worse than Eve, or Adam, in his callousness and harshness. Maybe we should not blame Eve at all, or Adam, for disobeying *a God like that*!

LOT'S DAUGHTERS, Genesis 19; THE LEVITE'S CONCUBINE, Judges 19

Like its counterpart story in Judges 19, Lot, the householder has male visitors, said to be *angels*. Lechers come demanding the visitors for sex. This is unthinkable to Lot. He could not hand over *male* guests in such a way: *females*, he *could*! He offers his two virgin daughters as substitutes, for the marauders to do with as they please. Luckily for the defenceless girls, the angels can perform miracles, and strike the licentious beasts with blindness. If the angels had stayed away in the first place, the two girls would not been in such danger - but then, we would not have discovered what a horrible father Lot was!

The poor girl in the Judges story fares much worse. No guardian angel, with supernatural powers to save *her*! *She* is thrown outside, like a piece of raw meat to dogs, is gang-raped all night, and dies. Although she, too, was a guest, she was *not* protected by the host, for she was only *female*, and did not count as a *guest*! What an insult to women these stories are!

The callousness of the Levite is evidently beyond the discernment of the writer, who has him say to the molested girl in the morning, "Get up. Let's go!" No "How are you?" No "Did they hurt you?" No "Are you still alive?" No wash. No breakfast. No guilt. No sympathy. Perhaps the poor girl was better off dead, than living with such an uncaring man! But why should *she* have been deprived of her life, in preference to the *man*, who was, after all, the one the attackers had wanted? It is all too disgusting for words, yet *two* such horrible stories are included in this so-called holy book, the Bible.

From a bad beginning, the tale gets worse for Lot's daughters, too. Visited by angels he may be, but he is a rotten father. Instead of looking out for his girls, and safeguarding a future for them by finding them husbands, which he could easily have done amongst Abraham's clan, he evidently decides he will let *them* look after *his* future, i.e. him. Despairing of being provided with husbands, the two decide, at least, to have children, and for this they use their drunken father. A sick, sick, story, in a book full of sick stories.

CANAANITE WOMEN

If *God* treated the very first, special and *only* woman as badly as he did, and God's *men*, their very *daughters* as badly as they did, what chance had the poor Canaanite women of any decent treatment from either God or "God's people"? *None!* True to form, if the women are not all done to death, it is only to keep the virgins for the pleasure of the Israelite men, from the king down. No matter that they had just experienced the most horrifying ordeal possible, siege and mass-murder of their tribes and families; no matter that they were grief-stricken at their loss, and in shock; they were sexually pure, and could be safely sexually abused (Numbers 31 v 18)! Pity the Canaanites: death or molestation is all they receive - and it is all thanks to the God of the Bible. It says so!

RUTH

This story is testimony to the unequal treatment by the two sides of each other, Israelite and Canaanite. Whereas the Israelites put the Canaanites to death, the Canaanites allowed Israelites to settle among them and intermarry. This is borne testimony to in the Samson and David stories, also. This is *hugely* significant, in assessing the character of the Canaanites, but the Church - *ignoring* it, in blind acceptance of the Israelite verdict - traditionally taught that the native people were fit only to be exterminated like vermin!

Time and time again, the Canaanites, in spite of the bad press the Bible *tries* to give them, *nevertheless,* are shown to be friendly, peaceful tribes. True to form, when there is a famine in the Land, the Israelites go to their friendly nonIsraelite neighbours, for food. This is the case in the story of Ruth, told in the book bearing her name. Elimelech, Naomi and their two sons move to Moab to escape the famine in Judah. They settle down, and the boys marry Moabite girls, Orpah and Ruth. The men die off, and Naomi is homesick. When she hears there is a good harvest again in Bethlehem, she decides to return there. The daughters-in-law start off on the journey with her, but she tries to persuade them to return home, remarry, and make lives for themselves with their own people. Orpah takes her advice, but Ruth, in love and devotion to Naomi and Naomi's God, sticks with her mother-in-law.

Neither of these Moabite girls is bad, nor can their nation possibly be construed as deserving the vilification of the Bible writings and Christian teaching. There is a fairy-tale ending to the story, when Ruth marries Boaz, eventually becoming the great-grandmother of David. Ruth might have decided to go home with Orpah, if she had known the destruction her great-grandson would inflict upon her generous nation (2 Samuel 8 v 2)! In the New Testament, Ruth is mentioned in the genealogy of Joseph (Matthew 1), tracing the line from Jesus back to Abraham through Joseph, even though Christianity denies he was Jesus' biological father! Again, Mary, being a *woman*, her genealogy did not rate a mention.

ESTHER

This is an interesting story from the period known as 'The Exile'. There were two invasions of the Hebrew kingdoms by powers which had a policy of transferring populations from one subdued area to another, presumably to disorientate them, and reduce the possibility of rebellion. Assyria had transferred the ten tribes of the northern kingdom, Israel, in 722 BC, and Babylon did the same to the southern kingdom, Judah, in 597 BC.

Many of these displaced Hebrews got on very well, it seems, in their new countries. Daniel was one such; he became a high-ranking civil servant. Esther, was another; she became a queen. Thus we learn a little about life in a harem! Whether the story has any historical basis, or whether it is entirely fiction is a matter of conjecture, but it is given a historical setting, and is the inspiration for the Jewish Feast of Purim.

The story begins in the royal palace at Susa. The powerful Emperor Xerxes is holding a banquet for all his administrators, and wine is flowing. After seven days of banqueting, the Emperor decides he would like to show off his lovely Queen, Vashti, wearing her (no doubt magnificent) crown. Queen Vashti does an unheard of thing: she refuses to appear! The whole Administration is scandalised. This requires a top-level conference to decide what is to be done.

It was unanimous that they could *not* let this insult to the Emperor go unpunished. If word of it got around, wives everywhere would think they could defy their husbands - "Well, Vashti does!" they would say. The very thought appalled the all-male Establishment. They made sure a *law* was passed. It was proclaimed throughout the Empire of Media and Persia, in all the writing systems and languages of every province, that men be *masters* in their households, and speak with final authority!

Vashti was lucky to escape with her life - *if*, indeed, she did. Probably she did not. A search was made for a beautiful maiden to take Vashti's place, and Esther, a lovely Hebrew girl, being brought up by her uncle, Mordecai, was chosen. Her uncle instructed her not to let it be known that she was Hebrew. She entered the harem, and Mordecai got a position in the Civil Service.

Mordecai learned of a plot to assassinate the Emperor. It was investigated, found to be true, and the conspirators were hanged. The matter was noted in the official records.

Then the evil Haman comes on the scene, as Prime Minister. The Emperor's order is that everyone should bow to this top official, as a mark of respect. Mordecai refuses, explaining that it is because he is Hebrew. The furious Haman determines to punish, not only Mordecai, but all the Hebrews throughout the Empire. He persuades the Emperor to go along with his dastardly plot to kill them, by telling him that there will be a massive contribution of silver into the Treasury coffers. The date for the massacre is set by throwing dice (purim). Instructions for it are sent all over the Empire in all the writing systems etc.

Mordecai is mortified at this development, of courrse, and dramatically and tortuously gets word to Esther to tell the Emperor he has been used in a trick to harm her people. Dramatically and tortuously, and laying her life on the line - for she could be put to death for daring to approach the Emperor, uninvited - Esther goes to him.

There is a magnificent build-up of tension to the climax of the story, where Esther, by holding a series of banquets for only two guests, Haman and Xerxes, is able to expose Haman as having plotted against her people - here she admits

71

to being Hebrew - and has the villain, Haman, strung up on the gallows he had prepared for Mordecai! Esther inherits Haman's property.

If the story had ended there, it would have been a masterly epic, but it continues, and the blood-spilling ruins it. *No* Hebrew was killed in the Empire, but Esther and Mordecai were able to arrange for the Hebrews, everywhere, to kill with impunity, whoever they wished, on an allotted day. They killed thousands of the Emperors subjects. She enjoyed the day of killing so much that she asked if they could have a *second* day of killing in Susa.

The story has degenerated into the usual gratuitous violence - a sickening pretext of revenge on people who had done nothing to deserve it!

This poem was inspired when The National Bible Society of Scotland held an Essay Competition for school pupils, in 1995, entitled THE RELUCTANT HERO, specifiying David or Esther as suitable subjects.

ESTHER, HERO?

Vashti, Vashti, *you* are *my* hero!
Modest, or just stubborn, why should you,
In all your beauty and splendour,
Appear before those leering, lecherous louts?
Had you no rights, Queen Vashti?

Queen - but *woman*, so a *slave*!
Every *man* in the Empire, prince or peasant, lofty or lowly,
Had more rights than you.

You were sacrificed to men's arrogance,
Put away for daring to stand up
Instead of being trodden underfoot.

What became of you, Vashti, my hero,
Banished, to be heard of no more?
Vashti, banished!
I question, and fear grips me, as my mind
Plays up and down the scales
Of the various possibilities,
And sombre chords strike my heart...

But what of you, Esther, good and obedient,
Subservient to men, so preferred?
Esther, chosen, and saviour of "God's Chosen",
Religious Esther, fasting and praying,
Clever and brave, doing God's will.

We grieved for you - then grieved again
To find your people
Going beyond the Law's decree,
Attacking, instead of defending,
Slaughtering, when no one was defying.

And we were ashamed for you, Esther,
Until you showed yourself in your true colours -
Until you showed us what you really were,
When you said, "Let us do again, tomorrow,
What we were allowed to do today.
Let us rejoice, and keep a feast - Purim!"
Esther, not hero, little Hitler, *butcher*!

And what of us,
Struggling to shake off, at long, long last
The shackles of indoctrination
Of Jews and Christians, down the ages,
Who told us *they* were *chosen*,
And Esther was *good*,
And Vashti was *bad*?

CHAPTER 19

THE IDEAL WIFE: Proverbs 31 v 10 - 31

This Bible passage is *the biggest insult* to women, craftily *concealed* in compliments. How many millions of Christians have had to endure the sanctimonious claptrap of sermonisers who did not discern this? Perhaps the *worst* example of such was a sermon, broadcast on BBC radio, from what used to be a college for priests, called Blairs, now closed. Of the multitude of texts and passages the preacher *could* have chosen, this priest, a man sworn *not* to take a wife, chose the passage named above! Thereupon, he uttered the usual praise of the disgraceful verses, claiming they gave Christian women a wonderful example to emulate, and lamenting, as he sided with v 10, that *none* of them ever measured up, and how *sad* that was, etc, etc.

The cheek of him! The nerve! Who was *he*, or who was the *writer*, or who is *any* preacher to deign to tell women that they never measure up to the standards that *certain selfish men* demand? For more than two millennia, worthy women have had these indignities showered on them from lectern and pulpit. "The spurns that patient merit of the unworthy takes", laments Hamlet - and how right Shakespeare was. He might have been writing about women and the Bible!

What this passage in the Book of Proverbs *really* is, is the ranting of a lazy, good-for-nothing-except-talk-husband, who wants a wife who will do *everything* for him, whilst he sits with other spoilt brats, demanding that women go on spoiling them!

He can turn on the charm when it suits him - "she is more precious than rubies" - but woe betide her if she ever needs a long lie one day! *All her life* she has to be providing *him* with wealth (for *she* will have *no* human or civil rights). She has not just to be busy working all the time, but she has to do it *eagerly*! She has to find fancy food to suit his delicate and gourmet palate. She is up preparing food, and organising the household, before daylight, whist *he* is still in bed! She speculates on property, making big profits, which she then invests wisely, making even *more* profit - for *him* - and I pity her if ever any of her investments fail! Not only is she clever, but she is also physically strong, so that she is able to "muck in" with the servants, and work long into the night - even though she has been working since before dawn! Not only does she spin, but she weaves her own cloth, making bedspreads and clothes, keeping her family warmly clad in winter, and herself looking like a model! And she makes enough of those, and other items, to sell. On top of all that, she is kind and generous to the poor.

74

When she speaks - which will not be often, if she is to keep pleasing the men - she utters only gentle words of wisdom. In the midst of, and in spite of, this exhausting round, with practically *no* time in bed, *still* this paragon of virtue, manages to have successful pregnancies, and bear children!

The verses that praise this woman ring very hollow indeed. *Cupboard love* is what it sounds like. How considerate would this man be if his wife were ever ill? There is no hint of compassion for this *slave*, grossly overloaded with work! True appreciation of her would mean that her husband would try to ease and share the burden of unrelenting toil and drudge. But he just sits there at the city gate, talking, bragging... "Will the children, who have been brought up to receive the best of everything, be any better than their spoilt father?" one wonders. I fear for this woman, if she were ever to slip for being *superwoman,* to being just *woman.* There is *no* respect here for woman, only for superwoman, and that *is not fair*! No one should be expected to be more than human.

The life of the good wife, in this chapter is, in fact, *very* like the life of women in many developing countries. They have a similar life of getting up before dawn, to fetch water, wood, and start preparing food for their families. They work hard all day, in spite of, in many cases, being pregnant most of their adult life. They have a short life expectancy. Many will die young of hard work and not enough rest. No one should say this is a good life, let alone an ideal one. Indeed, there are many agencies, thank goodness, whose function is to try to *end* this oppression *and exploitation* of women (to give it its true description).

This Bible passage should be *eschewed* by the Church, as violating human rights by praising a *distorted* view of women as work and sex slaves. It is *destructive* of a proper view of women, for, as a member of the human race, each person, irrespective of gender, should be *valued as an individual*. The Church needs to admit that the writers of such texts were not the nice, normal men, it has pretended they were, but were of the variety of male chauvinists, who have traditionally dominated religion, *and despised women*. Women have been second-class citizens, both in the Church and in the world, for too long, and it should *not* be tolerated in Christianity, just because their oppression was once the (evil) norm in society, or because it is still the norm in some societies.

This is to apply Liberation Theology to the passage.

CHAPTER 20

THE PROPHETS

The prophets listened to their conscience, and were unhappy with the injustice and oppression in their society, a society which was totally dominated by religion. And this religion, says Christianity, introduced the world to God, and produced Jesus Christ, the Saviour of the World. The world *needed* and *still needs* to be saved, it teaches, because *in Adam* it died - or is under sentence of death. Old Testament religion, however, showed a way of coming closer to God. That way was by performing rituals and offering sacrifices. Blood and the smell of roasting flesh were what kept its angry God appeased. Jesus' death on the Cross was in the tradition of blood sacrifice for sin, the full and final *sacrifice* to this angry God.

The above summary of the relationship between Judaism and Christianity shows that the prophets were not necessary to either religion; each could exist happily without them: sacrifice could atone for sin: morality was not required - as long as the animal sacrificed, or, in Christianity, the *person* sacrificed, was unblemished.

Fortunately, some of the Israelite population saw through the religion which said you could be close to God, whilst you cheated and oppressed, as long as you paid your Temple dues. The prophets saw that *the religion stifled conscience*. The religion let people *do* evil and *feel* good - *close to God,* even! "Bring me no more vain oblations...cease to do evil; learn to do well..." (Isaiah 1 v 13 - 17); "I desired mercy, not sacrifice", (Hosea 6 v 6); "I hate, I despise your feast days... Though you offer me burnt offerings and your meat offerings, I will not accept them... But let judgment (justice) run down as waters, and righteousness as a mighty stream!'(Amos 5 v 21 - 24)

Likewise, Christianity could perform the *mass*, and send armies to *massacre*, on *Crusades* (a contradiction in terms, since the *Cross* was supposed to bring *peace* with God and with one's fellow man). But the idea of "Holy War" was in the "Holy Book", and Christianity had not discerned that going to war was *never* holy, and must be *anathema* to God! The prophets were *no* help in this regard. *They* thought war was fine, even a godly tool!

Religion without morality is a sham. The prophets could see that. This is also what Jesus had to say, but, instead of concentrating on his *message*, Christianity got carried away seeing him as foreshadowed in the Old Testament, with *forms* and *parallels*, *analogies* and *types*. By becoming preoccupied with Christ's *blood* being shed, the *sacrificial lamb*, Christianity forgot the Sermon on the Mount, and the Parable of the Wheat and Tares - just as Judaism had forgotten The Ten Commandments, especially the one that said, "Thou shalt *not* kill".

In addition to being revered for putting moral content into Judaism, the Old Testament prophets have high esteem in Christianity for prophetic utterances, which the Church interprets as referring to Jesus and an everlasting reign of peace. Isaiah 2 gives rise to the kind of Zionism, embraced by Christianity, where the Temple in Jerusalem becomes the centre of the world, that every nation looks to, and comes to, for just settlement of disputes. Chapter 2 v 4 is sentimentally quoted in speeches and sermons, and engraved on walls at places like the United Nations, "And they shall beat their swords into ploughshares, and their spears into pruning-hooks. Nation shall not lift up sword against nation, neither shall they learn war any more."

This is rich - coming from two religions that went blazing trails of devastation through peaceful lands, raining down total destruction on countless nations, slaughtering friend and foe alike, men, women and children alike - *they* can sound so peace-loving! They insult us by their self-styled spiritual superiority - spirituality without morality! They *talk* about peace, after they have got as much as they can grab of lands and goods by war! We should not listen to warmongers who talk peace. They sermonise about peace from their pulpits of pillage!

About *peace*, we should ask the victims of war. In the Bible, that means we should consider the innocents invaded, hounded to death, usurped. What would the *Canaanites* think of those verses about beating swords into ploughshares?

They could only think, "What *kind* of God tells people to do to *anyone* what was done to us?" The only *moral* answer to such a question is, *"No God!"* Only some kind of *evil aberration* could inspire what was done in the Bible to the Canaanites. "Swords into ploughshares?" Why did they bring swords to Canaan in the first place? They must have been mustering an *army* when they *claim* to have been building a Tabernacle for God! This grisly story of God choosing a people to go out and kill others, in opposition to all known morality, *even their own*, has to be a *lie* - at best, a *delusion*.

Yet, the prophets are hidebound in the delusion that Israel, God's Chosen, will yet rule the world, as we read in Joel 3 v 9 - 10. *These* verses are *not* so apt to be quoted by the Church, however. Joel's prophecy here calls for the *opposite*

77

of Isaiah's - "Prepare for *war*. . . Beat your ploughshares into swords, and your pruning-hooks into spears!" This warmongering God is doing it again to the indigenous people, who had *the audacity to fight back* in the 5th or 4th century BC! Well, "Good for them!" I say. "They, had just cause." Such a prophecy inspires Zionism, and seduces Christians into Zionism, with Joel's prophecy ending, "for the Lord lives in Zion".

Christianity, whether deliberately or inadvertently, has created throughout the world, a sympathy for Zionism, the political movement which demands Palestine as a Homeland for Jews from all over the world - with few rights or safeguards for the indigenous people. Deluded Christians support Zionism, because of their blind acceptance of an evil theology, which murdered the original inhabitants of the Land. Now this same evil theology disregards the injustice it brings on the indigenous people of Palestine. They have been so contemptuously disregarded by the West - nations indoctrinated with the Old Testament content in their Christian teaching - that the Allied Powers gave away the Land of Palestine, in 1948, to foreigners who asked for it! Even to give away their *own* Lands, negotiators have not the right (or power) to do, because their *own* populations would object. How could they, then, have the *right* (they obviously had the *power*, through armed forces - power which they could not use on their *own* nationals) to give away *another* people's Land? Why the contempt for people *who had fought on their side*, the Palestinians, to whom they had promised Independence? Because of the *conquest of Canaan in the Bible* - for Christianity, completely lacking moral sense and discernment on this matter, blindly accepted the biased writings of the sanctimonious conquerors, inspired by a terrifying and terrorising *travesty* of God!

Such morality as the prophets tried to introduce into their religion was *limited* to the nation of Israel. Certainly, they made pronouncements about, against, and even sometimes in favour, of other nations - that God would not spare them, or that God would allow one or other of them to prevail against Israel *for a spell*, never permanently. God would make sure that Israel ruled in the end, OK! Compassion for widows and orphans, was only for *Israel's own* orphans and widows, *not* for those orphaned and widowed *by* Israel - of whom there was an enormous number, although *not* as many as *corpses*! Justice was for those who usurped the Land, *not* for those whose Land was usurped! The morality of the prophets did *not* go far enough. As Jesus put it, "Love your *enemies*. If you love only those who love you, what virtue is there in that?" (Luke 6 v 27, 32)

The morality of the prophets is welcome, for, at least, they point out the worthlessness of religion without it. Unfortunately their vision is limited by

78

their view that Israel is indeed 'The Chosen People of God,' with a God-given right to take what territory it wants, both in Canaan and beyond, and put whole nations to the sword. This is not morality enough. Justice has to apply to everyone, and not just one group which demands, demands, demands.

Liberation Theology must now be applied, both to the Middle East, and to the Bible - for Israel has returned to the Land of Palestine, claiming it has a Title Deed to that Land - the Bible! It has not! It is a false title deed.

CHAPTER 21

INDOCTRINATION

It feels like a bad day, when the penny drops that we have believed a lie, accepted the unacceptable, justified the unjustifiable. It *feels* bad, but it is, in fact, *good*. It is the beginning of putting things *right*, for we cannot put them right until we realise they are *wrong*.

Yet, it is only the beginning of a long journey. Escape from the familiar set of beliefs we have been brought up in, and ideas opposed to those that our friends and family are still entrenched in, is not straightforward or easy, and the journey requires resolve and energy, if we are to see it through. Even though the journey is not a physical one, but mental, it takes a lot of effort, and sometimes courage, depending on the degree of authoritarianism we are escaping from. To rethink all we have been taught is a strenuous exercise. To work out the new boundaries of our beliefs demands dedication to the task. It is easier to shut our eyes to the open door in front of us, that, in the name of intellectual honesty, we have to go through - but we should not ignore the niggling doubt, or turn away from the ray of light that showed us the darkness of our present position. To move from the twilight zone we have lived in for so long, into the light of day, is our duty to ourselves - to our intellect and to our character.

"What *me?* Indoctrinated? *Never!*" We *think* we have been taught only the truth. We forget how we stifled our little doubts, and uncomfortable reactions and questions long ago. We are sure that everything we have been taught, is eminently reasonable, and is what we *want* to believe. *That is the subtlety of it!*

So, what is this *lie*, that I, as a Church member, was taught and believed? What is the Church teaching that is so *unacceptable*? What is so *unjustifiable*? It is that God is a murderer, a monster, who chose a nation, whom he blessed, and told to massacre others, and teach the world thereby how to be *moral*, and how to be *holy*. That is the lie. That is unacceptable. That is unjustifiable.

How is it that such things have been believed in the church for two thousand years? It can only be that Christians have continued in the Old Testament teaching of the first Christians, who were Jews - accepting the unacceptable, and justifying the unjustifiable.

So, what does the Church have to replace those doctrines with? It has The Sermon on the Mount, with its exaltation of the poor and the oppressed. What

80

does it put in place of Jesus the Sacrificial Lamb, whose blood was shed for the remission of sins? It puts Jesus' teaching on the love and mercy of God. There was no need to hurt animals to put right human sin, any more than there was to hang Jesus on a Cross to put right the whole of the created order. It never fell in 'The Fall of Man'! Even *if* Adam and Eve had existed, and even *if* the scene in the Garden of Eden had taken place, it was *good judgment* to eat the fruit, and thus become *capable of moral action*, rather than remain zombies, never knowing right and wrong. *Good* and *right* are not virtues based on *ignorance*, they become virtues only when there is the exercise of moral choice. Indoctrination tends to remove choice from those held in its sway. It equates morality with blind obedience to what leaders say, and immorality with questioning them.

But *do* question! It is the means of escaping indoctrination. It brings liberation.

REFERENCES

THE BIBLE   King James Version

GOOD NEWS BIBLE   The Bible Societies; Collins

THE HITCH HIKER'S GUIDE TO THE GALAXY
                                         Douglas Adams, PAN BOOKS

LES MISERABLES   Victor Hugo, LE LIVRE DE POCHE

JUNIOR PRAISE   Marshall Pickering

THE BIBLE IS GREEN (COMPETITION 1992)
                               National Bible Society of Scotland

TO A MOUSE   Robert Burns

ADAM LAY YBOUNDEN   Anon. 15th c

MR NOAH BUILT AN ARK, H167, Junior Praise   Marshall Pickering

MATTHEW HENRY'S COMMENTARY ON THE NEW TESTAMENT
                                        Hodder & Stoughton

OTHELLO   William Shakespeare

THE RELUCTANT HERO (COMPETITION 1995)
                               National Bible Society of Scotland

ORDERING

For further copies of this book, or others in this series
ask at your local bookstore, or write to:
MARION BOOKS
P.O. Box 28207
EDINBURGH
EH9 1WL

POST & PACKING

Please add 60p for the first book ordered
and 30p for each additional bookordered.
Up to a maximum of £3.00 for U.K. orders.

For overseas orders,
add £1.00 per copy for Europe and £2.00 for elsewhere.

PAYMENT

Make all cheques, postal orders etc, payable to: MARION BOOKS
For credit cards:

Card Type:...

Card Number: [| | | | | | | | | | | | | | | |]

Expiry Date:..

Signature:...

For your postal address - PLEASE USE BLOCK CAPITALS

Name:...

Address:...

....

....

....